ISLAM

YOUNIS TAWFIK

ISLAM

KONECKY & KONECKY

Translated by Amy Huntington.

All quotations from the Qur'an from *Al-Qur'an*,
translated by Ahmed Ali. Used by permission
of Princeton University Press.

Konecky & Konecky
150 Fifth Ave.
New York, NY 10011

ISBN: 1-56852-189-8

Layout by Studio 31

Printed and bound in Italy

Because of the numerous books currently available on Islam, one may think that there is nothing left to say about the subject. Nevertheless, if we consider that every religion represents human consciousness, that it reflects human nature and thoughts, we must conclude that all religions evolve, even when they seem immutable.

Islam, in particular, encompasses the essence of the human being to the point of becoming an everyday philosophy. Inseparable from life and social context, it is therefore continually evolving.

In the literal sense of the word, Islam means submission to the divine will; the root of the word also expresses the idea of peace and uprightness of the soul. The Muslim intensely lives the relationship with his creator through a religious practice that touches each moment of his existence. In effect, the *shari'ah* (the Islamic law, the path that leads to God) is a foundation of the religion that concerns the social as much as the private dimension.

A religion as staunch and intense as Islam will inevitably provoke discussion, particularly in its confrontation with the West. Nevertheless, the meeting of the Islamic world with the contemporary West has not consisted solely of conflicts. In the past, Islam has made important contributions to the development of European civilization. The modern era, marked by colonialism and the birth of independent Islamic states, is extremely complex. There exists much confusion between what is, and what is not, Islam.

This illuminated and universal religion, which is widespread across vast regions and characterized by great cultural differences, has experienced internal confrontations of many different, and sometimes debatable, interpretations.

Thus, there is still a need for books which explain in a simple and objective fashion (especially for those looking in from the outside) the history, the beliefs, the religion, and, more generally, the everyday life of the followers of Islam. I appreciate the editor's choice of a Muslim author for the book, of someone born and raised in the Islamic culture. It is my hope that this makes the book more credible in the eyes of the reader. At the same time, it has given me a new opportunity to reflect upon my own religion, in order to write of it more freely and enthusiastically.

Page 2: *Prayer in the courtyard of the Giblan Mosque.*

Left: *The palace of Muhammad surmounted by seven heavens. Persian miniature from the 18th century. Bibliothèque Nationale, Paris.*

Historical Survey

The Arabs before Islam

The Qur'an defines Arab society predating Islam by the term *al-jahiliyya* (ignorance), referring as much to the polytheism of the time as to the existence of habits and customs that Islam rejects. In spite of this pejorative qualification, the era before the Islamic revelation is considered by the majority of historians to have been an artistically rich period in the history of Arab civilization. It was also an epoch to which we owe the creation of several towns which became important centers of culture and commerce. The Arab people, of Semitic descent, are divided into two lines of descendants: "Qahtân" and "Adnan." From their origin, they occupied southern and northern Arabia respectively but were later united into one people through migration. From the eighth century BCE, southern Arabia was a region rich with several highly developed civilizations, such as those of the Manaeans, Sabaeans, and Himyarites. In contrast, until the advent of Islam, the population in the north was preponderantly nomadic. Civilization was found primarily in the caravan centers or in buffer states maintained by bordering empires. An example of this is Iraq, which was protected by Persia and Syria, and maintained as a Persian satrap — and successively conquered by Alexander the Great, the Romans, and the Byzantines. The Arabic language, developed among these nomadic tribes in the solitude of the desert, belongs to the Semitic family of languages.

Left: *Saudi Arabian countryside, the same now as it must have appeared before the advent of Islam.*

Below: *A dromedary in the desert, a method of locomotion which was central to the nomads of northern Arabia.*

Previous pages: *A man prays in the desert.*

Arabs. The term "Arabs" appears in Assyrian texts as early as the first millennium BCE, to describe the nomads of the deserts and steppe of northern Arabia and Syria. During the Greco-Roman epoch, the term was applied indiscriminately to all peoples of the Arabian peninsula.

It was later adopted by the Qurayshi tribe, of which the Prophet was a member. The first written documentation of the language, a stele discovered at Hegra, bears a date corresponding to the year 267 CE and also contains inscriptions in Nabataean, Aramaic, and Thamudaean.

Migration of Peoples

To better understand the ethnic, linguistic, and cultural development of the Arabian peninsula, one must imagine a time in which the Arab peoples were in perpetual movement throughout the territory. The Semitic-speaking peoples were forced by the progressive desertification of the peninsula to search for more hospitable settlements on the fringes of the desert. The first to leave the peninsula were the Canaanites, who moved toward the eastern coast of the Mediterranean around 3,000 BCE. In the second millennium BCE, the Akkadians also abandoned the peninsula, establishing themselves in Mesopotamia. They were followed by the Amorites, who settled along the arc of the Fertile Crescent, and later by the Aramaeans. For millennia the peninsula also welcomed Semitic-speaking peoples coming from the fertile regions of the north. Caravan trails of great commercial importance criss-cross

The Tigris. The Fertile Crescent, lying between the Tigris and Euphrates rivers, was the historical cradle of the first large civilizations.

Egypt.
Over thousands of years, the language and writing of ancient Egypt changed profoundly. Hieroglyphics and demotic writing were used until the first centuries of the common era, at which time Coptic began to replace them.

Syria and Mesopotamia. The dominant languages in these countries were of Semitic origin, the oldest being the Akkadian languages, including Assyrian and Babylonian. The Canaanite languages include Biblical Hebrew, Phoenician and its

derivative called "Punic". At the beginning of our millennium, most of the dominant languages in this region were replaced by others, all deriving from the same root. Phoenician was still spoken in the seaports of Syria and in the North African colonies; Hebrew was the language of

the peninsula, attesting to the existence of products for export and merchants. They required methods of transport adapted to the desert, such as the dromedary, which was domesticated around 3,000 BCE.

The Arabs rapidly developed their agricultural, commercial, and, above all, military techniques. Arab contingents mounted on dromedaries had been fighting for different armies since the beginning of the first millennium BCE, principally in the northern regions.

During the first centuries of the common era, central and southern Mesopotamia, with Ctesiphon as its capital, were firmly held by the Persians. The northern region was claimed on one side by the Romans and Persians and on the other side by local dynasties. Mesopotamia was at times considered a part of Syria. During the reign of Emperor Constantine (r. 311–337), the Christian religion was imposed throughout the Roman empire, accompanied by the progressive Christianization of the state.

Another important event in this time was the movement of the capital of the Roman empire from Rome in the West to Constantinople in the East. In its new capital, the empire survived one thousand years after the fall of Rome under the shock of

Herd of dromedaries. Detail of a miniature by Iraqi artist al-Wasity (1237). Bibliothèque nationale, Paris.

Below: *Detail of a Qur'an in Kufic script (between the 8th and 9th centuries). Biblioteca Ambrosiana, Milan.*

religion, literature and science; and Aramaic, the language of commerce and diplomacy, spread throughout the Fertile Crescent, Persia, Egypt and the region corresponding to present-day southern Turkey.

The Arabic language. At the beginning of the common era, it was primarily spoken in the center and north of Arabia. Another Semitic language deriving from Ethiopian was spread through the southeastern regions by settlers from southern

Arabia to the Horn of Africa. The penetration of Arab-speaking peoples into the south of Iraq and Syria diffused this language through the entire region. With the Islamic expansion of the seventh century, the Arabic language virtually replaced Aramaic.

Buildings and tombs dug into the rock at Petra, the ancient capital of the Nabataeans, in Jordan. The town was a stopover on the route to the east and to south Arabia.

barbarian invasions. The Hellenization of the Middle East (begun by Alexander the Great and carried on by his successors in Syria and Egypt) was continued by the Roman government and the Christian church. The Middle East also witnessed unending wars between the two great powers of the era: the Persians and the Byzantines. Their continual rivalry is the dominant theme of the region's political history until the dawn of the Islamic caliphate. These conflicts were not due uniquely to territorial claims. To these warring powers, the control of commercial routes was of extreme importance. The most direct route from the Mediterranean to the Far East passed through territories under Persian control. The trade of goods such as Chinese silk and herbs and spices

from the East Indies and Southeast Asia — of vital interest for Rome and later for Constantinople — was threatened by the Persians, who cut off the routes and held caravans for ransom. Struggle between the two empires was a permanent state of affairs since each wanted to be the dominant power in the region.

In the year 25 BCE Emperor Augustus attempted to conquer the territory corresponding to present-day Yemen in order to gain control of the southern coast of the Red Sea. The expedition took a disastrous turn, which convinced the Romans to permanently abandon

Persians and Byzantines. Ardashir (226–240CE), founder of the Sassanid dynasty, led a series of military campaigns against Rome. His successor Shapur I (240–271) succeeded in capturing the Emperor Valerian, who died in prison.

Petra. The first political contact between the Romans and the peoples of the desert dates to the year 65 BCE, the date of Pompey's visit to Petra, the capital city of the Nabataeans. This people, probably of Arab origin, were nevertheless

Aramaeans by culture and written language. Petra was a very important caravan city on the route from India to southern Arabia, as well as acting as a buffer-state between the Roman provinces and the desert.

any attempt to penetrate into the Arabian peninsula. The caravan towns and the small city-states surrounding the desert were left to bear the responsibility for protecting their own commercial activities and securing their own strategic bases.

In this manner, a number of towns and border kingdoms were born and developed. The most important of these were Petra, Palmyra in the Syrian desert, and Hatra in the present-day Iraqi desert, several kilometers to the south of ancient Ninevah. Hatra was overpowered by the Roman emperor Trajan after an attempted rebellion. Although the empire was expanding eastward, the immense Arab territory still remained beyond Roman control. This was not the case, however, at the frontiers, where numerous city-states and small kingdoms were springing up — either as allies with, or protectorates of, the Parthian empire to the east and of the Roman empire to the west. Rome's policies, evolving from a "good neighbor" strategy to one of annexation, affected the states of Palmyra and Petra and altered the relationships between regional powers.

The situation changed once more after the campaign for power by the Sassanians in Persia. Practicing aggressive politics, they embarked upon the conquest of several kingdoms on the border of northeast Arabia. Toward the middle of the third century, they

Archaeological site of Palmyra, in Syria.

Below: *Bas-relief showing Zenobia, Queen of Palmyra. National Museum, Damascus.*

Zenobia. Near the end of the 3rd century, Queen Zenobia attempted to re-establish Palmyra's independence. The attempt was crushed by an army dispatched by Rome, and the city was re-incorporated into the empire.

15

Detail of a bas-relief in stone of the Sassanid period of Naqh-i-Roustam, in the Fars region (southwestern Iran). These imposing bas-reliefs celebrate the actions of the monarchs of the Sassanid dynasty (224–651).

Below: *Image of the Syrian desert.*

returned to the east coasts of Arabia, where they jeopardized local stability. They destroyed Hatra, a territory that had been annexed by the Romans.

From the fourth to the sixth century, the Arabian peninsula suffered from widespread impoverishment. Arab chronicles tell of an economic crisis that ravaged towns and of the rise in nomadism, which occured at the same time as the decline of agriculture and fixed settlements. This crisis was not unrelated to the events that were taking place at the peninsula's northern borders. During the fourth century, an extended period of peace between Rome and Persia made the long and costly caravan trails through the desert less appealing. Many caravan towns, which had sprung up along the commercial routes, were abandoned, thus contributing to the return to nomadism.

The decline of commerce and trade also resulted in a decline in living standards and cultural development. This crisis had repercussions that even affected the southernmost towns of the Arabian peninsula: many tribes had to emigrate north in search of more fertile pastures.

At the beginning of the sixth century, the Byzantines and the Persians resumed their conflict, plunging the region back into a state of endemic war. However, the struggle was beneficial to the Arabian peninsula, offering it an advantageous role in the midst of the turmoil. The Byzantines, who were wary of their rivals, began searching for routes outside of territory controlled by Persia. The southern route to India had once again become attractive and took on considerable importance.

The Arabian peninsula. This is a high plateau of steppe and deserts surrounded by mountains. At the center stretches the desert of Nafud. The southern zone is called Rub' al-Khali, (the Empty Quarter.) To the west, the Hijaz mountain chain, known as the barrier, was crossed in the past by caravan routes linking the Mediterranean with the Indian Ocean. The Hijaz separates the coastal strip called Tihâmah from the immense central high plateau, the Najd, (the raised land). To the south, a

As the two empires competed for the alliance of those tribes who hoped to profit from traffic along these routes, the kingdoms and frontier city-states re-established their previous position.

It was in this context, around 527, in an attempt to weaken the Sassanians, that the Byzantines provoked a conflict between two Arab kingdoms: Ghassan, a Byzantine protectorate, and Hira, which was under the protection of the Persian empire. As the maneuver was not sufficient to thwart Persian influence in the region, the Byzantines attempted to subjugate the neutral city-states, to assure their supremacy and commercial monopoly over the entire coast of the Red Sea.

On another front, the Byzantines incited the Christian nation of Ethiopia to rise up against the Jews of Yemen, who were under Persian protection. The Ethiopian troops, recently converted to the Christian faith, attacked the peninsula by sea, destroyed the last remaining independent state of southern Arabia and opened the country to Christianity. In 570, their campaign towards the north brought them as far as Mecca, an important caravan city and place of pilgrimage for Arabs. The expedition was, however, a failure. Ultimately, the Persians regained control of Yemen.

The temple of Hatra, in Iraq. During the first centuries of the common era, some towns in Mesopotamia were occupied by peoples of Arab origin.

chain of high mountains stretches from Yemen to the Gulf. The climate encouraged agricultural development and the production of spices and incense, resources highly valued by the civilizations of the Mediterranean basin.

Ghassan and Hira. Ghassan, a town under Byzantine protection, was located to the northwest of the desert, at the approximate site of present-day Jordan. To the northeast, under Persian protection, the town of Hira prospered. Both Arab kingdoms were of Aramaic culture and Christian religion.

The military maneuvers of this period and the migration of peoples to the frontiers of the Arabian peninsula had lasting cultural and religious consequences. The majority of Arabs who lived in the region's neighboring areas — those areas annexed by the Byzantines or under the control of Persians — were Christians. Other Christian settlements were found in southern regions, such as Najran and Yemen, where Christians lived alongside large Jewish communities originally from Judea. These Jews settled principally in Yemen and in the numerous towns of the peninsula.

During this period, the non-Arab communities became completely "Arabized." However, very few Arabs adopted the Persian religion, Mazdaism. This religion was not readily accesible to outsiders. Elsewhere, a large number of individuals called *hanif* began to appear. The word derives from an Arab term designating those who, while rejecting polytheism and adhering to the Abrahamic idea of one God, have not truly adopted another religion.

From the oral tradition, we possess a relatively clear idea of the structure of pre-Islamic Arab society. Tribes were founded on blood relationships. Each member identified himself as *banu*, son of the line whose name he bore. Although relations between tribe members were fundamentally egalitarian, a certain form of hierarchy, according to personal worth and eloquence, was recognized. From the decision-making council of the elders, emerged the figure of the *sayyid*, lord, elected for his noble qualities, courage, charisma, and ability to conduct debates. However, families reserved

Oral tradition.
For cultural, linguistic and historical reason, the doctors of Islam began from the eighth century to gather the testimony of the oral tradition, predating and contemporaneous with the Revelation. If writing was already known, it was seldom used, and the collection consists mainly of orally-transmitted poetic works. Through rhythm and rhyme, poetry made the task of memorization easier. It is a veritable receptacle of customs and of the way of life of these societies. Poetry functioned as a mirror for a group, fiercely attached to its independence, at the same time contributed toward the strong cohesion of the people, ensuring its subsistence and survival. During the *samars*, long evening gatherings, the poets sang of the people's

the right of retaliation when offenses were committed against their members, and this challenged the coherence of the group.

The harsh conditions of desert life did not offer the Arab peoples much latitude in their choice of artistic materials. If the culture's most refined form of art was the spoken word, it is because that art form is not dependent upon tools or materials.

Flexible in nature, oral tradition compensated for a deficiency in other artistic practices. Its suppleness permitted it to express the nuances of emotions and to evoke the instability of everyday life. During this time, the life of the bedouin was completely conditioned by his desert surroundings; his imagination and emotions were shaped by his environment. In short, the experience of the desert was the formal structure of the bedouin's sensibility, constituting what one could call a collective unconscious. Arab art was like the changing and ephemeral physiognomy of the desert. Its mission was to describe the appearance of things, their metamorphoses, and the mobility of perceptions.

Nomads in the Syrian desert: an encampment of bedouins. Nomadism allowed for only one form of art — that of the spoken word.

traditions, and genealogies. They extolled the glory of the tribes, the chiefs, and the nobles, and decried their enemies' weakness and villainy, whether genuine or supposed. The oral tradition was spread through the desert by singers, *rawi*, who traveled from tribe to tribe. Their participation at periodic gatherings, (the most famous one was held at Ukaz near Ta'if, in the Hijaz) also helped to propogate the tradition. This oral patrimony, which was transcribed at the beginning of the Islamic era, remains a unique witness to the history of this people and of their religion.

Muhammad the Prophet

According to tradition, the patriarch Abraham led Hagar and their son Ishmael to a desolate valley south of the land of Canaan. An angel announced that Ishmael would give birth to a large nation there, and in this valley Hagar saw water spring from the sand. The valley would become a stopover for caravans crossing the desert, because its water was sweet and abundant. The wells there came to be called Zamzam.

One day when Abraham was visiting his son, God showed him the precise spot near the wells where he and Ishmael were to build a sanctuary. God explained how it was to be constructed: the name of the building, deriving from its shape, would be Ka'bah, cube. The four corners were to point to the four cardinal directions, and the most holy object, a black stone from the heavens, was to be set into the building facing west. A great pilgrimage to the Ka'bah, instituted by Abraham, was to take place once a year, but other, less important pilgrimages, could take place at any time. Over the centuries, throughout Arabia, a growing number of pilgrims surged towards Mecca.

Little by little, the purity of the religion of the One God became lost. Even the wells of Zamzam disappeared, for which the members of a tribe from Yemen, the Giurhum, were responsible. The descendants of Abraham tolerated their growing dominion over Mecca, since one of Ishmael's wives belonged to this tribe. But the Giurham committed such heinous crimes that they were finally expelled from the city.

Left: *Muhammad ascends to Paradise on his winged horse. Beneath are the Rock of Jerusalem and the Ka'bah. Persian miniature of the 16th century.*

Below: *The name of the Prophet. When it is written or pronounced, it is always followed by the formula* Sâlla i-Lahou 'alihi wa sâlam, *"May the blessings and peace of Allah be upon him." Detail of an inscription on ceramic.*

The Angel. In the desert, Hagar and Ishmael were stricken with thirst. Fearing for her son's life, Hagar climbed onto a rock in hope of finding water. Seeing nothing, she climbed higher, but in vain. Distracted with fear, she ran back and forth seven times, until, exhausted, she sat down to rest. An angel then appeared to her and commanded her to stand up and take the child in her arms. He told her that God had ordained that Ishmael's descendants would give birth to a great nation. When she opened her eyes, Hagar saw a spring flowing from the sand under the heel of her child.

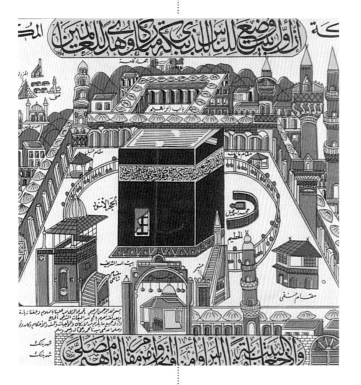

Popular print depicting the Ka'bah. A sheet of black brocade completely covers the building. The four corners are placed facing the four cardinal directions.

Before fleeing, they filled in the wells with part of the treasure of the sanctuary and concealed them by covering them with sand.

In turn, the Khuzas, an Arab tribe descended from Ishmael, emigrated to Yemen and, returning to the north, became the rulers of Mecca. They made no attempt to find the wells, and they introduced a Syrian idol, Hubal, into the Ka'bah.

Around the fourth century, a descendant of Abraham named Qussay, a member of the Arab tribe of Quraysh, married the daughter of the chief of the Khuza. At the death of his father-in-law, Qussay governed Mecca and became the steward of the Ka'bah. He had four sons, of whom his favorite was 'Abd al-Manaf. Even so, Qussay chose his eldest, but much less gifted son, 'Abd al-Dar, to succeed him. His decision provoked dissension that flared up in the next generation. A group of the Quraysh gathered around the son of 'Abd al-Manaf, Hashim, who was the most respected man of his time. As violence was strictly forbidden, not only in the sanctuary but also within several kilometers radius of Mecca, the two factions reached a compromise. The son of 'Abd al-Manaf retained the right to collect taxes, with which he would provide food and drink for the pilgrims, and the son of 'Abd al-Dar was entrusted with the keys to the Ka'bah and granted other privileges as well.

Hashim. The son of 'Abd al-Manaf was very skilled in business matters. It was he who initiated the two great caravan voyages mentioned in the Qur'an: one toward Yemen, and the other toward the regions of northwest Arabia, Palestine and Syria.

Pilgrimage. Once the Ka'bah was completed, God ordered Abraham to institute the rite of pilgrimage to Mecca: "'Associate no one with me, and clean My House, for those who will circumambulate it, stand (in reverence), and bow in homage. Announce the Pilgrimage to the people...'" (Qur'an 22: 26-27).

Along the caravan route, eleven days by camel from Mecca, lay the oasis of Yathrib, inhabited by Jewish tribes but governed by an Arab tribe from the South. This tribe had quickly divided into two clans that lived in perpetual conflict: the Banu Aws and the Banu Khazraj. Hashim married the most influential woman of the Banu Khazraj. Their son, 'Abd al-Muttalib, exhibited leadership qualities from a very young age. At the death of his uncle, the young man was judged the most worthy to take charge of nourishing the pilgrims.

'Abd al-Muttalib was respected by the Quraysh for his courage, intelligence, generosity, and charisma; but he had no sons — a serious detriment in Arab society. He prayed to God for male offspring, adding a vow of supplication: if God sent him ten sons, he would sacrifice one at the Ka'bah. His prayer was granted, and when his sons were grown, he gathered them together and told them of his pact with God, exhorting them to help him keep his vow. He took them to the sanctuary, where each of them gave him an arrow in order to draw lots between them.

The arrow of the youngest and best loved son, 'Abd Allah, was chosen. But the women of his family persuaded 'Abd al-Muttalib to consult a soothsayer in Yathrib, the

Circumambulation of pilgrims around the Ka'bah. According to the Qur'an, God himself ordered Abraham to establish the rite of the pilgrimage to Mecca, one of the five pillars of the Islamic faith.

The Wells of Zamzam. Near the northwest portion of the Ka'bah is a site called Higr Ishmael, because the tombs of Ishmael and Hagar lie under its stones. Abd al-Muttalib often slept in the Higr, in order to remain close to the House of God. One night he had a vision of a creature who showed him how to find the wells of Zamzam and ordered him to uncover them and dig them out. With the discovery of the wells, the buried treasure of the sanctuary was recovered. 'Abd al-Muttalib's skill and courage enabled him to avoid combat between the clans. This earned the clan of Hashim the appointment as the guardian of the wells.

'Abd al-Muttalib whispers in the ear of the elephant. Turkish miniature. Topkapi Saray Museum, Istanbul.

Below: *The elephants miraculously stop before the Ka'bah. Topkapi Saray Museum, Istanbul.*

town of his birth. The soothsayer counseled him to draw lots between the life of the young man and ten camels, the blood price in Mecca. At the tenth draw, the arrow finally fell on the side of the animals. Therefore, in place of the young man, 'Abd al-Muttalib sacrificed one hundred camels. Such was the will of God, and the life of 'Abd Allah was spared. His father decided to find him a wife. A niece of Qussay was chosen: the beautiful Aminah, daughter of Wahab. Their marriage was celebrated in 569, the year before that which came to be known as the Year of the Elephant.

The Birth of Muhammad

In 570, 'Abd Allah joined a caravan going to Palestine and Syria. On his return, while in Yathrib with his grandmother's family, he fell ill and died soon afterwards. There was much grieving in Mecca. The only consolation for his father and wife was the birth of his son a few weeks after his death. The child, immediately presented in the sanctuary and in the House of God for a ceremony of grace, was named Muhammad.

Though few Arabs of the time were literate, noble families sought to teach their sons to speak perfect Arabic. Eloquence and rhetoric were considered virtues, and the worth of a man was measured by his talents as a

The Year of the Elephant.
In 570, Yemen was under Abyssinian domination, and an Abyssinian Christian named Abrahat al-Achram was viceroy. His ambition was to compete with the supremacy of Mecca as center of pilgrimage, by building at San'a' a sumptuous cathedral. This provoked the anger of Arab tribes, who attempted to desecrate it. Abrahat, enraged by this provocation, swore to raze the Ka'bah in retaliation. He gathered an army, putting an elephant at its head. Only divine intervention was enough to prevent the destruction of the Ka'bah. God sent a multitude of birds who dropped stones on the troops, until the army of Abrahat was forced to retreat.

poet. The tribe of Quraysh, having only recently settled in towns, were accustomed to entrust their children to Bedouin wet nurses. The young Muhammad was given to a nurse named Halimah. She raised him in the outdoors according to the custom of the desert, on the principle that children benefited from the freedom of spirit that it was believed to bring. He lived in this way for three years. At the age of six, his mother took him to visit her parents in Yathrib. During the voyage, she fell ill and died a few days later. His grandfather took the orphan into his charge, pouring upon him all of the love that he had felt for his dead son, Muhammad's father. Two years later he died as well, and Muhammad was entrusted to his uncle, Abu Talib.

As this uncle had many children and lived in poverty, his nephew felt obliged to contribute to his maintenance. He took the flocks of sheep and goats to graze in the hills near Mecca, where he passed long periods in solitude.

Muhammad was allowed at a very young age to accompany his uncle on his travels. When he was ten years old and travelling with a caravan to Syria they encountered a Christian monk named Bahira in Bostra. Bahira knew of the prophecies in ancient manuscripts that spoke of the coming of a prophet among the Arabs. Upon seeing the child and observing his features, the monk realized that he was in the presence of the Prophet. He informed Muhammad's uncle of this, enjoining him to keep the secret.

Because of his poverty and contrary to the custom of Arab society, Muhammad remained unmarried for a long time. Marriage between cousins was the accepted practice of the time, and the young man had asked for the hand of his cousin Umm Hani, but in

The birth of Muhammad. Detail of a Turkish miniature of the 13th century. Topkapi Saray Museum, Istanbul.

The purification.
Tradition recounts a very significant episode in the early life of the Prophet: the purification of his spirit when he was only three years old. Behind the tents of the camp, Muhammad was playing with his foster brother when two men appeared, dressed completely in white, bearing a golden basin full of snow. Seizing the child, they laid him on the ground, opened his chest and took his heart out in their hands. They found a small black lump that they cast away. Then they washed his heart and chest with the snow and let him leave. Muhammad's wet nurse, alarmed by the story of the Prophet's brother, who had witnessed the scene, decided to bring Muhammad back to his family to protect him.

The installation of the Black Stone into the rebuilt Ka'bah. Edinburgh University Library.

vain. Because of financial reasons and clan alliances she was, however, given in marriage to another relative. Nevertheless, among the richest merchants of Mecca, there was a woman, Khadijah bint al Khuwaylid, of the powerful Assad clan, and a distant cousin to Hashim's children. Following the death of her second husband, she began hiring men to take care of her commercial affairs. Khadijah knew Muhammad's reputation in Mecca, where he was called *al-amin* (the trustworthy), and she decided to entrust him with merchandise she was sending to Syria. Upon his return, Muhammad went to her house with the goods bought with the profits of his sales. Although fifteen years his elder, Khadijah was very beautiful. Attracted by the young man, she asked one of her friends to arrange a marriage. The day of the wedding, Khadijah gave her husband a young slave, Zayd ibn Harithah, who became Muhammad's adopted son. To help his uncle, Muhammad took his cousin 'Ali into his home. That year, the Quraysh decided to rebuild the Ka'bah. Muhammad was given the responsibility of placing the Black Stone inside.

The retreat

Fond of solitude, Muhammad often withdrew to meditate in a cave on Mount Hirah near Mecca. He was now in his

The young Muhammad. At the age of twenty-five, Muhammad was a man of medium stature, thin and broad shouldered. His beard and hair were black and slightly wavy and his skin light. His forehead was high and his eyes large and almond-shaped (black according to some descriptions and brown according to others), bordered with very long lashes.

Muhammad's children. Muhammad's marriage with Khadijah was happy. But their first son, Qasim, died before he was two. Four daughters followed: Zaynab, Roqayya, Oumm Kolthum, and Fatima. A second son, 'Abd Allah was born, but he also died at a young age.

fortieth year. One night during the month that would later be called Ramadan, he was alone in the cave, having vowed to fast and to carry out a spiritual retreat. Suddenly an angel appeared to him and ordered him to read the parchment that he carried. Terror-stricken, Muhammad fled, and, returning to his house, he recounted the event to his wife. Khadijah went to consult her cousin Waraqah ibn Nawfal, a *hanif* who knew the ancient writings. He announced to her that her husband would become the prophet of his people. Waraqah's affirmation was confirmed by the evidence of revelations coming directly from God. Encouraged by his wife, Muhammad began speaking of the angel and the revelations to those who were closest and dearest to him. The first to accept the teachings of the new religion after Khadijah were his cousin 'Ali, his adopted son Zayd, and the faithful friend of the Prophet, Abu Bakr as Saddiq, a well-loved and respected man. Following Khadijah's example, Abu Bakr did not hesitate to sacrifice all of his wealth to the cause of Islam. Thanks to him, many others adopted the new religion. The number of believers — men and women — quickly grew, even though no public call to convert to the new religion had as yet been made. In the first days of Islam, the Companions of the Prophet went in a group to pray unobtrusively in the valleys on the outskirts of Mecca.

Gift of a city to the Prophet. Miniature from Tabriz, 14th century. Topkapi Saray Museum, Istanbul.

The reconstruction of the Ka'bah. Until the time of its reconstruction, the Ka'bah was without a roof, and its walls were, at their highest, the height of a man, permitting intruders too easy access. The reconstruction caused serious discord among the Quraysh, since each clan claimed the honor of returning the Black Stone to its place. Muhammad found a way to resolve their dispute. Calling for a blanket, he spread it on the floor and placed the Stone in the middle. He then had a member of each clan grab hold of the blanket and lift it together. Once the blanket had been lifted, he took the Stone himself and put it in place. The construction could then be continued, and the Ka'bah was finally completed.

Gathering of Arab merchants. Miniature from the Avicenna Codex. Biblioteca Ambrosiana, Milan.

Idolaters would surprise them and attack them with insults. But the Muslims decided to abstain from violence as long as God did not condone it.

When Muhammad first proclaimed the birth of the new religion, the Quraysh seemed prepared to tolerate it. But when they understood that the religion was directed against their gods, their traditions, and their principles, they feared for their commercial activities. A few of them went to Abu Talib to ask him to put a stop to his nephew's activities. Seeing that their pressure had no effect on the Prophet, the Quraysh began persecuting those believers who could not protect themselves.

The origins of the community

Despite the increasing hostility of the Meccans, the number of believers continued to grow. For the first time, the Prophet himself was attacked and insulted openly by the

worst enemy of Islam, Abu l-Hakam who, out of contempt, the Muslims have named Abu Jahl (the father of ignorance). The Prophet merely rose up and returned to his home. Hamza ibn al-Muttalib, an uncle of the Prophet, having learned of the incident, went into the sanctuary where Abu Jahl was seated with several Quraysh. With all of his force, he hit him on the shoulders with his bow, while proclaiming before all his adherence to Islam. In order to avoid the worst, Abu Jahl

The Revelation.
When the angel appeared to Muhammad, his first word was, "Read!" When Muhammed responded, "I don't know how to read," the exhortation was repeated twice: "'Read in the Name of your Lord who created, created man from an embryo; read for your Lord is most beneficent, who taught by pen, taught man what he did not know.'" (Qur'an 96: 1-5).

The first believers.
Among the first converts were two cousins of the Prophet, Ja'far and Zubayr, followed by others. In a verse of the Revelation, the Prophet was ordered to convert his clan, but he met with little success.

refrained from reacting. This new victory of Muhammad alarmed the Quraysh, since the conversion of Hamza, a respected warrior, meant reinforcement and protection for Islam.

Following this episode, the Quraysh decided that they must act quickly to stop a movement that endangered their interests. One of them went to see the Prophet. Finding him seated alone near the Ka'bah, he offered many enticements, which Muhammad rejected, refusing to make any concessions. He continued to win the adherence of influential believers, like 'Uthman ibn 'Affan, a rich and respectable member of the Umayyad clan of 'Abd Chams, and other young Quraysh whose arrival strengthened the community. The Prophet soon realized that even if he himself were protected, many of his disciples would become victims of persecution. For their security, he ordered them to take refuge in Abyssinia, where they received a warm welcome. He granted them complete freedom to practice the religion as they saw fit. A group of twenty-four people participated in the first emigration of Islam.

In the meantime, though an attempt to oppose the flight to Abyssinia had failed, the persecution of the Muslims who stayed in Mecca increased. Abu Jahl's nephew, 'Umar ibn al-Khattab, who, until then, had been one of the fiercest opponents of the Muslims,

Hamza strikes Abu Jahl for insulting the Prophet. Persian miniature (1030). Bibliothèque nationale, Paris.

Aws and Khazraj.
At Yathrib, the two tribes of Banu Aws and Banu Khazraj were constantly in conflict. Each sought to forge an alliance with the Jewish tribes living in the oasis. They met only with mistrust, since the Jews showed little tolerance toward the polytheism of the Arabs. When the Arabs of Yathrib learned that a man had proclaimed himself the Prophet of Mecca, they decided to ally themselves with him. The head of the Banu Aws sent a delegation to obtain Qurayshi support against the Banu Khazraj, but in vain. The Prophet tried to offer them something more precious than the alliance they sought. He recited to them a part of the Qur'an, but they resisted his message.

29

The Prophet lays the foundations of the first Islamic mosque at Kubah near Medina. Turkish miniature of the 16th century. Public Library, New York.

himself converted to Islam. A courageous man, he did not hesitate to pray publicly in front of the Ka'bah and to exhort other Muslims to join him. In 619, at the age of sixty-five, Khadijah died, and Abu Talib, the uncle of the Prophet soon followed her to the grave. The grief in Muhammad's soul intensified, endangering his role as Prophet. The same year, however, the Prophet wed a thirty-year-old widow, Sawdah bint Zam'ah, and several months later, the daughter of Abu Bakr, the young and beautiful 'A'ishah, was promised to him in marriage. In 620, during a pilgrimage, in a place called al-'Aqaba, near Mina on the route to Mecca, the Prophet met six men from Yathrib, of the Banu Khazraj tribe. These men subsequently decided to submit themselves to Islam's precepts.

Meanwhile, the fourth and most violent conflict between Banu Aws and Banu Khazraj broke out in Yathrib. Its indecisive outcome resulted in a temporary truce. The six Khazrajites who had met Muhammad at al-'Aqaba carried his message to their clan. During the summer of 621, five of them returned on pilgrimage, bringing with them seven other men, two of whom were from the Banu Aws tribe.

They drew up a pact with the Prophet, which came to be called the pledge of al-'Aqaba. One year later,

The persecutions. The conversion of his nephew, 'Umar, did not persuade Abu Jahl to discontinue his persecution of the Muslims. An edict was proclaimed, commanding the Quraysh to abstain from marrying the women of the Hashimite clan, giving their daughters in marriage to the Hashimites, and selling or buying from them. Forty of the Qurayshi leaders placed their seal on this agreement, some under duress, and the document was solemnly placed in the Ka'bah. The edict against the Muslims continued for two years but was never very effective.

seventy-three men and two women renewed this pact, encouraging Muhammad to urge his disciples to emigrate to Yathrib. His closest followers, with the exception of Abu Bakr and his cousin 'Ali, abandoned Mecca.

Hijrah, the emigration

Finally, because the Quraysh were conspiring to take his life, the Prophet fled Mecca along with Abu Bakr. After many difficulties, they reached the oasis of Yathrib on September 27, 622. Upon his arrival, Muhammad was welcomed with a great celebration. He immediately ordered that an interior courtyard be purchased and transformed into a mosque.

The Prophet called the Muslims of Yathrib, *ansar* (supporters), while naming his followers from the Quraysh and other tribes *muhajirun* (exiles). The two communities gained support from a third: a treaty of alliance was made by the Prophet between his disciples and the Jews of the oasis. They founded a unique community of believers, based on a mutual respect for their different religions. In this way, Islam established itself firmly in the oasis, which soon changed its name to al-Madinat al-Mounawara, the Enlightened Town. When the construction of the mosque was completed, the Prophet added two small houses to the east side, which he occupied with his daughters and his wife Sawda. He celebrated his marriage with the young 'A'ishah soon afterwards.

The revelations of this period were concerned predominantly with legal matters: the establishment of the fast of Ramadan, the obligatory almsgiving, and the distinction

Zaynab, one of the daughters of the Prophet, leaves Mecca to join her father in Medina. Turkish miniature. Turco-Islamic Museum of Art, Istanbul.

The assassination attempt.
The Quraysh agreed on a plan suggested by Abu Jahl to assassinate the Prophet. Each clan was to choose a trustworthy young man. At an agreed moment, they would all attack the Prophet at the same time. In this way, the guilt for his blood would fall upon all of the clans. The conspirators planned a meeting at nightfall near the Prophet's house. But Muhammad and his cousin 'Ali caught sight of them in time. Muhammad asked 'Ali to lay down on his bed and wrap himself in his green cloak to fool the aggressors. Under cover of darkness, and thanks to divine protection, the Prophet managed to escape and fled to Yathrib with Abu Bakr.

The mihrab *of the Mosque of al-Azhar. The* mihrab, *the niche which indicates the direction of prayer, originally pointed towards Jerusalem. It was turned towards Mecca following a revelation which took place in Medina during the month of Sha'ban, in 624.*

between what was forbidden and what was permitted. But shortly after the arrival of the Prophet to Medina, a revelation (in response to the situation the new faith found itself in) granted Muslims the authorization to fight. War against the polytheists of Mecca now became inevitable. The incident that unleashed the first battle was an unsuccessful attack against a Meccan caravan, but there were many other reasons for conflict. The Muslims were driven to battle because of their desire for vengeance, the confiscation of the emigrants' goods for the Meccans' profit, and the increasing economic pressure placed upon the *ansar*, who were responsible for the maintenance of the community. The Prophet advanced with an army consisting of about 350 *ansar* and *muhajirun*. He stationed them at Badr, west of the coastal route which runs from Syria to Mecca, in the hope of ambushing the caravan of Abu Sufyan, the head of the Umayyads, allies of the Quraysh. But Abu Sufyan evaded the trap by taking an indirect route. Meanwhile, a Qurayshi army was dispatched to his aid. On March 17, 623, the Quraysh, with a powerful army of one thousand men, confronted the Muslims. It was a hard-fought battle and the Quraysh lost several of their best horsemen and clan chiefs. Driven back, they retreated to Mecca. Two major battles between the Muslims and the Quraysh followed. Though victorious in 625, the Quraysh were decisively beaten in the attack against Medina in 627.

The following year, the Prophet decided to accompany his followers on the pilgrimage to Mecca. Learning of the plan, the Quraysh called a meeting of their assembly. Though the sacred month had begun, they sent two hundred horsemen to cut

The battles
During the two years following the Battle of Badr, the Meccans suffered from the closing of the caravan routes bordering the Red Sea. In the attack on an important Meccan caravan on its way to Iraq, a precious cargo of money and various merchandise was hijacked. This disaster persuaded the Quraysh to accelerate their preparations for the war that they had begun following the defeat at Badr. The battle, which took place at Uhud, to the north of Medina, was a stinging defeat for the Muslims and ended in a massacre. Many relatives and Companions of the Prophet were killed, but despite this terrible blow suffered by the community, Muhammad maintained his resolve. In 627, the Quraysh decided to launch

off the pilgrims' path. A battle was avoided when the pilgrims changed direction and reached the pass running to al-Hudaybiyah, a plateau located below Mecca, within the boundary of the sacred territory.

Wishing to resolve this delicate situation, the Quraysh sent one of their men, Suhayl ibn Amir, known for his political adroitness. The negotiation resulted in a pact that established a ten-year armistice. It was agreed that for one year the Prophet and his followers would not enter Mecca against the wishes of the Meccans, nor in their presence. However, whoever expressed the desire to join forces with the Prophet would be free to do so. The following year, the polytheists were obliged to leave Mecca for three days so that the Prophet and his disciples

The Battle of Badr (624), fought between the supporters of the Prophet and the idolaters of Mecca. Topkapi Saray Museum, Istanbul.

Below: *Medinan warriors. Detail of a Turkish miniature of the 18th century. Museum of Turco-Islamic Art, Istanbul.*

could carry out the pilgrimage in their absence. One year later, in accordance with the treaty, almost two thousand Muslims carried out the rite of pilgrimage in a town deserted by its inhabitants. Some time later, around 630, a nocturnal raid by the Quraysh against a tribe allied with the Prophet resulted in one death. Muhammad considered that this incident marked a rupture of the armistice. Unable to accept his allies' attempts to avoid conflict, he ordered preparations for a campaign against the Quraysh. His army, the largest ever to have emerged from Medina, was almost ten thousand men strong. The

a decisive attack against Medina and, with the aid of their allies, raised an army of nearly four thousand men. But the siege failed and the Qurayshi army was forced to retreat.

The army of Zayd ibn Harita. Three months after the success of the pilgrimage, the Prophet sent a mission of fifteen ambassadors to an Arab tribe within the borders of Syria. All but one of the ambassadors were killed. Muhammad then recruited

an army which he entrusted to the command of Zayd, his adopted son. Zayd's army faced a coalition of the tribes of the north and of rallied Byzantine forces. The Muslim troops withdrew to Muta in the south. The battle was lost.

Muhammad is host to Christian monks during a voyage in Syria. Turkish miniature from the 16th century. Museum of Turco-Islamic Art, Istanbul.

Prophet divided it into four units, each with its own commander. They invaded Mecca from four directions and took the city. Muhammad celebrated his victory with a solemn entry. Leading the cortege, he went first to the Ka'bah, then to drink from the wells of Zamzam. Finally, he returned to the Ka'bah, where he gave the order to destroy the paintings and the idols inside.

After the Muslim victory over Mecca, the Prophet returned to Medina and began receiving delegations from all of the regions of Arabia, as well as ambassadors from the Jews and Christians of Yemen and Najran. The Prophet informed them that the rules of Islam demanded that respect be shown to the messengers sent to collect taxes to which the Muslims, Christians, and Jews were subject. He added that the protection of God and the Islamic state would benefit themselves, their goods, and their sanctuaries. The following year, the Prophet left Medina on pilgrimage at the head of more than thirty thousand men and women. He firmly established the rite according to the ancient Abrahamic rules and preached a sermon which he concluded with the question, "O men, have I loyally transmitted my Message to you?" Upon receiving an affirmative response, he lifted his finger to the sky and

The impostors.
In a Christian tribe of Yamamah, recently converted to Islam, a man named Musaylimah pretended to be a prophet. He sent a letter to Muhammad with a proposal to divide the power. Muhammad responded to him that power belonged only to God, as the earth belonged only to Him. After short period of success, Musaylimah was assassinated by his own disciples.

said: "O, God, be witness!" At the end of the pilgrimage, the Prophet returned to Medina, where he soon faced another danger to Islam: impostors who claimed to be prophets.

The Death of the Prophet

One day, as Muhammad was preparing to go to prayer, he was stricken with an agonizing headache. The next day, June 8, 632, he went to the mosque. The prayer had begun, and Abu Bakr, who was leading it, wanted to give him his place, but Muhammad signaled him to continue, saying, "Lead the prayer!" Returning home to 'A'ishah, he stretched out on her bed, laying his head on his wife's chest. She heard him enunciate the words, "O God, to Paradise with the Supreme Presence." His head became heavier. 'A'isha laid it on a cushion, and she, with the other wives, began crying.

The Muslims had to decide quickly who would assume authority over the community. Abu Bakr had been the closest Companion of the Prophet and had led the prayer when Muhammad was still alive. Before the gathered community of believers, 'Umar took the hand of Abu Bakr and swore to him his loyalty, as did all who were present. In Medina, the grief was great, and a crowd of inhabitants gathered to pay a final homage to the Prophet and pray for him.

Tomb of Muhammad at Medina. Turkish ceramic from the 18th century. Museum of Turko-Islamic Art, Istanbul.

The disbelief of 'Umar. Misinterpreting a verse of the Qur'an, 'Umar refused to believe that the Prophet was dead. He proclaimed in the mosque that Muhammad had withdrawn into the Spirit but would soon reappear among them.

Abu Bakr. Abu Bakr was not present at the death of the Prophet, but he quickly returned and took decisive control of the situation. He gave a speech in the mosque that made a deep impression on those assembled. After having praised God, he declared with authority, "O people, whoever adores Muhammad, may he know that Muhammad is truly dead. Whoever adores God, may he know in truth that God is living and will never die!"

The Islamic state

At the time of Muhammad's death, different languages were being spoken in the region corresponding to the present-day Middle East; different religions were professed, and authority was divided between several monarchs. Within a short time, emerging Arab power, armed with a new faith, had overturned the established political and military order. Islam became a state religion. Arabic, the language of the Qur'an, was carried by military conquest, although it did not become the official language until much later. The Islamic state founded by the Prophet benefited from the reign of four *al-Khulafa' ar-Rashidun* (the Rightly-Guided Caliphs) — the vicars, successors, or lieutenants of the Prophet.

The first task that faced Abu Bakr was the defense of the unity of the state and of Islam, which were menaced both by the *riddah* (secession) of tribes who refused to pay tribute to Medina, and by dissension caused by false prophets. Abu Bakr reacted with firmness, and in 633 the secessionist movement was crushed.

The Arab forces were ready to carry their faith across the desert to the more developed civilizations of Mesopotamia and Asia. In 636, under order of the caliph, Muslim troops penetrated Palestine and Transjordan. Meanwhile, other troops attacked Hira, the ancient residence of the Lakhmids on the Euphrates, in Mesopotamia, placing the predominantly Aramaic-speaking Christian population, long Persian subjects, under the rule of the new Islamic state. By caliphal order, the commander Khalid ibn al-Walid, whom the Prophet had named Sayfu l-Lah (the broadsword of Islam), left Iraq in order

Beyond the desert. In the beginning, due to the progressive impoverishment of the soil of the Arabian peninsula, the Arab expansion was motivated by the desire to obtain new territories and vital resources. Inflamed by the strength of the religious conviction instilled in them by the Prophet and by the pride they felt in being agents of a powerful and unifying belief, the Arabs did not fear confrontations with the Byzantine and Persian armies who were better prepared and equipped.

Left: *Mosaics in the Umayyad baths. Palace of Khirbat al-Mafjar, Palestine (8th century).*

Below: *Abu Bakr, the first caliph after the death of Muhammad and one of the four to be called "the Rightly-Guided." Detail of a Turkish miniature. Topkapi Saray Museum, Istanbul.*

Detail of a minaret sculpted with inscriptions in Kufic characters. Saveh, Iran. With the birth of the Islamic state an architecture developed which would use calligraphy, in particular Kufic calligraphy, as an ornamental element.

to assist troops in difficulty in Syria, beginning his legendary march across the desert. After a rapid series of successes, the Muslims made their entry into Damascus in 635. In August 636, a decisive battle against the troops of Heraclius took place on the Yarmuk, a tributary of the Jordan. This victory put Syria into Muslim hands. The capitulation of Jerusalem followed in 636, as well as that of Caesarea, the last bastion of the Byzantines in the region, in 638. In 634, 'Umar ibn al-Khattab began his ten-year caliphate, a decisive period for the formation of the Islamic state and for the collective memory of orthodox Islam. The Muslim success against Syria was followed by victories over Persia. In 636, after three days of violent combat, the Muslims won the Battle of Qadisiyya, in southern Iraq, which opened the route to the capital, Ctesiphon. The last Sassanid monarch, Yazdagird, was defeated at Diyala and again at Nihawand, near Hamadhan, in 641. The towns and fortresses of the high Iranian plateau fell one after the other. But almost ten years passed before the Arabs secured control of the region.

At the end of 639, on 'Umar's order, several thousand Arab horsemen crossed the Egyptian border. The Byzantine defense was weak. Alexandria surrendered, and her Coptic-speaking Christian people, having lived under Byzantine hegemony for centuries, passed under Islamic domination in 645.

'Umar ibn al-Khattab. Appointed by the dying Abu Bakr, 'Umar was named caliph with the agreement of the majority of the Companions and was able to govern without opposition. During his caliphate he succeeded not only in consolidating the empire, but also in laying the foundations of a well-ordered and effective political administration. 'Umar is attributed with the decision to begin the Islamic calendar with the *hijrah*.

The spread of Islam. Following the Arab conquest, the Persians embraced the message of Islam and greatly contributed to the spread of the faith among the peoples of Central Asia.

The Islamic state extended religious tolerance to its new subjects, a policy which had been enunciated in the Law as well as in pacts established between the Prophet and the Jews and Christians — 'ahl al-kitab (the people of the Book). Security, freedom of religion, and the right to protection were guaranteed to Christians and Jews in exchange for payment of a poll tax, the *jizya*, and a land tax, the *kharaj*. Muslims were only obliged to pay *zakat* (the almsgiving tithe).

'Umar did not nominate a successor but instead chose a *shura*, a council composed of six of the Prophet's oldest companions, to select a new caliph. His elected successor was 'Uthman ibn 'Affan, the Prophet's son-in-law, of the Umayyad clan, and the first member of the Meccan aristocracy to have joined Islam. During the twelve years of 'Uthman's caliphate (644–656), territorial expansion continued. Persia and Armenia were entirely subjugated, while in North Africa, Arab armies advanced upon Tripoli and present-day Tunisia.

The unrestrained nepotism of 'Uthman and his seizure of the contributions collected from abroad created opposition from the clans. The revolt spilled over into the provinces, and, as far away as Iraq and Egypt, insurrectionary groups marched on Medina. 'Uthman was finally assassinated.

The room of the Umayyad palace of Khirbat al-Mafjar, Palestine (8th century). The building, for the most part destroyed, is an important witness to the architecture of the epoch. The palace and the mosque had large interior courtyards showing Byzantine influence.

Taxes. Aside from the almsgiving tithe owed to the state, Muslims did not have to pay any taxes. The entire weight of taxation resed on the peoples subjugated to Islamic rule. Later on, it became necessary to create a complex administrative and financial organization to collect revenues in the conquered countries and pay the army. This organization was founded on registers, or lists of soldiers, the *diwan*. It was managed by an *'amil*, a civil servant who worked alongside of a political and military governor, the *wali*.

The tributes levied by the new state were paid to the *baitu l'mal*, the State Treasury of Medina which the caliph personally managed.

The Umayyad Great Mosque at Damascus.

The civil wars

The door to the caliphate was finally open to 'Ali, Muhammad's cousin, but first he had to combat the opposition led by 'A'ishah, the widow of the Prophet, and then by Mu'awiyah ibn Abi Sufyan, the governor of Syria, who wanted to obtain compensation for the death of 'Uthman and to seize the caliphate. With the raising of 'Ali 's army, the politico-religious schism of the Kharijis developed that would deprive 'Ali of the chance

of governing in peace. Five years of a turbulent reign ended tragically with his assassination in 661. A group 'Ali's followers formed the Party of 'Ali, or *Shi'ay at 'Ali*, known later as Shi'a. Its followers are called Shi'is.

After 'Ali's death, his eldest son Hasan abandoned his claim to the caliphate in order to support Mu'awiyah, who had already been declared caliph in Syria. The emergence of the Umayyad dynasty began a new period in the history of Islam.

The Umayyads, whose dominion extended from India to Spain, confronted the moral and military resistance of the Shi'a and of the Kharijites, whom they had fought against during 'Ali's reign. The Shi'a claimed affiliation to the imamate, an equivalent of the caliphate, which belonged by divine right to the descendants of the Prophet's family. This was the beginning of the second

The Umayyads.
Lacking authority, 'Uthman was unable to resist the pressure of his noble Umayyad cousins, eager to seize power. One of them, Mu'awiya, son of Abi Sufyan, conquered Cyprus (649) and then pressed forward to Sicily. In 655,

the Byzantine navy met Mu'awiya's new Arab fleet off the coast of Lycia in their first naval battle. The Muslim victory foreshadowed their dominance over the Mediterranean region.

The definitive version of the Qur'an.
One of the principal achievements of 'Uthman, successor of 'Umar, was that he ordered the canonical recension of the Qur'an (650).

civil war, which would have great religious importance. Husayn, the youngest son of 'Ali and grandson of the Prophet, headed the revolt, which broke out in Iraq. He and his followers were exterminated by the Umayyads at the Battle of Karbala, in October 680. Only his young son escaped alive. It was following this massacre that the Shi'a party, a political movement from the very beginning, found its religious dimension. Beseiged, stormed, and burned, Mecca was not spared during the rebellions.

Unity of the Empire

In 685, 'Abd al-Malik ibn Marwan, from another branch of the Umayyads, rose to the throne. During his reign, he re-established the unity of the empire. We owe to him, and to his successor Hisham, the foundation of the imperial organization. Arabic became the official language of the administration, replacing Greek and Pahlavi. 'Abd al-Malik minted gold coins, ornamented with Arabic words.

The empire expanded under the reign of al-Walid (675–715). In 711 Arab troops crossed the strait of Jabal-al-Tariq (Gibraltar) and conquered Spain. In 704, during the attempted invasion of Transoxiana, starting from northeastern Iraq, al-Walid's army was stopped by the Turks, first at Samarqand, and then at Bukhara. It was during this time that the Arabs penetrated Indian territory for the first time, by way of southern Persia. One of the last great Umayyads was Sumar ibn 'Abd al-'Aziz (717–720), the Pious Caliph, known for his profound religiosity and his scrupulous sense of justice.

In the east, the Hashimites, who were supporters of the party of 'Ali's' descendents, had plotted in order to assert their rights. Profiting from the new rebellions against the

'Abd al-Malik ibn Marwan.
His caliphate saw the beginning of construction of monumental religious edifices, symbols of the universal message of Islam, such as the Dome of the Rock and the Aqsa Mosque, built in 692 on Temple Mount in Jerusalem.

The treasure room in the courtyard of the Umayyad Great Mosque of Damascus. The octagonal edifice, supported by columns, is decorated with mosaics.

Below: *The Dome of the Rock at Jerusalem.*

The inner courtyard of the Fortified Palace at Ukhaydir, Iraq. It was constructed in 778, not far from Baghdad, by Isa ibn Mussa, a nephew of al-Mansur.

Umayyad power, Abu al-'Abbas, a descendant of al-'Abbas, uncle of the Prophet, proclaimed himself caliph. The Umayyads and their followers were massacred. The only surviving member of the dynasty succeeded in conquering Spain, where he established himself as Abd ar-Rahman I. In Arabia, the center of power was transferred to Syria, nearer the Mediterranean and in North Africa to Iraq, gravitational center of the large cosmopolitan empires of the ancient Middle East. Abu Dja'far al-Mansur (d.775), who succeeded his brother Abu al-'Abbas, was the true founder of the dynasty of 'Abbasids. He laid the foundation of the first Islamic metropolis, Baghdad, on the eastern bank of the Tigris, near Ctesiphon.

In al-Mansur's government, the management of the provincial administration was entrusted to an *amir*, who acted as military commander and oversaw the financial and fiscal services for the *amil*. Each province of Baghdad had its *diwan* (register).

The governor carried out the call to Friday prayer, which helped strengthen his position as head of the region's Islamic community. This consolidation of political, religious and military power led to decadence and corruption. In conformity with the strictures of the *shari'ah* (the Islamic Law), the judiciary power was exercised by the *qadis* (judges), appointed directly by the

The 'Abbasids.
During the 'Abbasid Caliphate, which started with Abu al-'Abbas, the privilege of being a member of the court was extended to Persians and other peoples. The patriarchal monarchy with its blend of political and religious power evolved into an absolute monarchy. The use of the Arabic language was imposed in the cultural and administrative domains, and artistic and scientific culture was at its high point. The lands owned by the Arabs benefited from fiscal privileges. The 'Abbasids ceased allying themselves only with aristocratic families; they also chose concubines and slaves of different origins as wives. This practice contributed to the disappearance of the distinction between Arabs and non-Arabs.

caliph. In cases of abuse of power and injustice, the people would appeal to them. The maintenance of public order was confided to the *shurta*, a locally-recruited police. It was under the reign of the 'Abbasids that the slow degradation of the empire began. Spain and parts of the Maghrib had acquired their independence in the eighth century. Other outlying provinces, in the east as well as in the west, followed suit.

The initiative of Iranization, which was started by al-Mansur, was expanded under his son al-Mahdi (755–785). Meanwhile, the caliphal court and the religious apparatus of theologians and doctors of the law became closely intertwined. The caliph, pure and firm in his defense of Islam, harshly suppressed Manichaeism.

The golden age of the empire which began with al-Mansur culminated in the long reign of Harun ar-Rashid (786–809). This was a period of well-being and social peace, due mainly to the competence of Iranian viziers (members of the Barmakid family) in the management of fiscal, political, and economic affairs.

However, their power was judged excessive by ar-Rashid, who reproached them for having unjustifiably augmented their family's wealth, at the expense of the state. After the tragic fall of the Barmakids in 802, the administration of the provinces, entrusted to an incompetent caliph, sustained considerable damage. It was during this period that the

The arch of the mihrab *of al-Hakam II, decorated with mosaics, in the Great Mosque of Córdoba.*

Below: *Detail of a painting on an Islamic ivory chest (7th–8th centuries). Museo del Bargello, Florence.*

Abu Ja'far al-Mansur. Under the caliphate of al-Mansur and his successors, the important function of *wazir* was exercised by the Persian Barmakid family. From then on, the ceremony of the court would be marked by Iranian influence. Based on the Persian model, a permanent army was created. Its soldiers were regularly enrolled in the registers, the *diwan*, and received a monthly wage. A permanent, salaried army allowed the caliph to be much less dependent on the Arab tribes.

The ritual fountain building in the center of the courtyard of the Mosque of Ibn Tulun at Fustat in Egypt, constructed in 876–879. The minaret stands to the left.

empire began to decline and weaken. Religious uprisings in the East and the loss of entire regions in the West ensued.

The Caliph ar-Rashid chose al-Amin, his son by a wife of noble Arab origins, as his successsor. He entrusted the government of Khorasan and the western regions to another son, al-Ma'mun, whose mother was a Persian slave. Furthermore, he named him as his brother's successor. But al-Amin, the new caliph, had no intention of respecting his father's wishes. This led to a bloody conflict between the brothers. In 813, Baghdad, al-Amin's capital, surrendered after a very long siege. Al-Ma'mun took the title of caliph but judged it prudent to remain in the western provinces for a while before returning to the capital.

Baghdad was now capital of the empire, but the Persian provinces' desire for independence resulted in the formation of small local kingdoms. In 820, a general of Iranian origin, whom al-Ma'mun had named governor of the region of Khorasan, obtained independence and founded his own dynasty. Other princes imitated him. The fame of the Caliph al-Ma'mun is very much linked to the support that he gave to philosophical, scientific

Harun al-Rashid.
Harun al-Rashid is perhaps the most famous caliph. Known for his magnanimity and his sense of justice, he inspired the legendary figure in the stories of *The Thousand and One Arabian Nights*. His prestige was recognized by the world's most important rulers, from the Emperor of China to Charlemagne, with whom he exchanged ambassadors and gifts. Within his kingdom, he reinforced the sacred character of his position as commander of believers by personally leading the Friday prayer in his capital and by planning pilgrimages to Mecca and *jihad* (war) against the unbelievers.

and medical research and to the creation of the *ayt al-hikma* (House of Wisdom), center of Greek and Syrian translation.

Al-Ma'mun was succeeded by his brother al-Mu'tasim (833–842). He added officers from Turkey and soldiers from the provinces of Central Asia to the army. The continual disturbances that these soldiers provoked obliged the caliph to transfer his court and his Turkish guard to Samarra. This imperial garrison city, 150 kilometers north of Baghdad, served as capital of the caliphate until 892, when one of al-Mu'tasim's successors decided to return to Baghdad.

The energetic al-Mutawakkil (847–861) re-established the caliphal hegemony. He checked the power of the Turkish guard, which had become uncontrolled, introduced the Mu'tazilite doctrine, and, with the support of both laymen and theologians, reinstated a strict orthodoxy. These measures, however, were not sufficient. In 861, al-Mutawakkil was assassinated by the Turkish guard. During the next nine years there were four caliphs, and the capital was overwhelmed by complete anarchy. In 870, al-Mu'tamid was elected caliph. Because of his young age, he was placed under the tutelage of his brother, Talhah al-Muwaffaq, who, in twenty years of government, recovered part of the caliphate's lost authority.

What had begun as an agrarian and military state had developed into a cosmopolitan empire with prosperous commercial and industrial activities, and towns that were magnets for labor and capital. But this transformation created inequalities, dissatisfaction and social tensions. As people were exposed to the great diversity of

The spiral minaret of the Great Mosque of al-Mutawakkil, Samarra, north of Baghdad (842–852). The Caliph al-Mutawakkil founded the garrison city of Samarra to accommodate his large army.

Below: *The Imam in the Mosque, miniature by al-Wasity (1237). Bibliothèque nationale, Paris.*

Al-Ma'mun. The Caliph al-Ma'mun, who was a member of the Mu'tazilite theological school, attempted to impose it as the official doctrine of the state. The Mu'tazilites founded a school of philosophy based on the application of rational thinking to orthodox religious dogma. Following this teaching, the imam granted himself doctrinal authority superior to that of the consensus of the doctors of the Law.

cultures and to an increasingly effervescent intellectual activity, a number of heretical movements emerged.

The Caliph al-Muktafi (902–908) succeeded in quelling the Karmatian revolts in Syria and Iraq, but the situation grew serious when other rebellions broke out in North Africa. His successor, the young al-Muqtadir (908–932), faced a new wave of Shi'i religious revolts led by the Ishmailis, who conquered the town of Kairouan. Their chief, 'Ubay d Allah, proclaimed himself caliph deriving his authority from his descent from Fatima, the daughter of the Prophet. He founded the Fatimid dynasty. Northern Syria fell under the control of the local Hamdanid dynasty, while in Persia a Shi'i family, the Buwayhids, took power.

Meanwhile, confusion and disorder reigned in Baghdad. In 945, when the Buwayhid Emir of Khorasan, invested by the 'Abbasid caliph with the honorable title of *Mou'izz al-Dawla* (Glory of the State), entered the capital to defend the dynasty, the power passed into the hands of the Shi'a. The army extended its influence, and a new and powerful military aristocracy arose. Meanwhile, the income from taxes continued to grow.

In North Africa, the Fatimid state annexed Egypt in 869 and extended its influence to Syria and the Arabian peninsula. In contrast to the Buwayhids, these Ishmailis refused to recognize the authority of the 'Abbasid

The inner courtyard of the al-Hakim Mosque at Cairo, and, to the left, the octagonal minaret. The Mosque was constructed by the Fatimid Caliph al-Hakim between 996 and 1021.

Social tensions.
At the end of the ninth century a caste of mendicants of multiethnic origins appeared in the country, while revolts of black slaves, the Zendjs, broke out in the salt marshes of southern Iraq, placing the state in jeopardy.

The Karmatian movement.
The brutal revolt of the Karmatians in 875 stirred up the peasants and the bedouins of Iraq. Though inspired by the Shi'i movement, its claims were essentially political and social. The revolt rapidly

won the frontier regions of Syria and Iraq and spread to a great part of the Arabian peninsula. This was the origin of the foundation of the State of Bahrain, which maintained its independence until 1075.

dynasty. Prosperity and solidity strengthened Fatimid Egypt, while the caliphate of Baghdad weakened. A series of external attacks hastened the fall of the empire. In Europe, Christian forces began to take the initiative in Spain and Sicily, an expansion that led to the Crusades. But the real danger for the Islamic empire came from the East. Waves of invaders were arriving from the Asiatic steppes. Among them was a Turkish people from the north of the Caspian sea that had converted to Islam in the tenth century and provided soldiers for the auxiliary troops of local rulers. In 1038, their chief, Tughril-Beg, of the Seljuk dynasty, proclaimed himself sultan at Nishapur, and embracing Sunni orthodoxy against the Shi'i power, marched upon Persia. In 1055, he entered Baghdad where he put an end to the Buwayhid regime. The caliph bestowed on him the title of sultan as well as the full power and responsibility to fight the Fatimids. For almost a century the Seljuks concentrated all of their efforts on the institution of the religion, on strengthening the power of the state, and on cultural development. Disturbances, plots, and the international situation weakened them, to the advantage of the Caliph al-Nasir (1180–1225). While the Ayyubids fought against the Crusaders in Syria and Egypt, the Kharezmchahs, in Iran, were captured by the Mongols who soon burst into the Muslim world. In 1243, they invaded Iran and then Iraq, devastating the 'Abbasid capital in 1258. The fall of the caliphate brought a great epoch of Islamic history and civilization to an end.

Genghis Khan receiving homage from dignitaries. Persian miniature from the 14th century. The most dangerous invaders for the caliphate of Baghdad arrived from the east. They later converted to Islam, becoming assimilated to the religion and customs of the lands they had invaded. Bibliothèque nationale, Paris.

Fatimid Egypt.
Under the Fatimid dynasty, tolerance of ethnic and religious diversity promoted a flowering of culture and inaugurated a golden age for Egypt and for the universalist dimension of Islam. With economic and commercial expansion, the urban centers multiplied and experienced true prosperity, giving birth to a cosmopolitan elite. Greek, Persian and Indian literary, scientific and philosophical works were translated into Arabic, contributing to the renewal and enrichment of Arab humanism.

From decadence to the reality of today

After the conquest of Baghdad, the Mongol commander Hulagu turned towards the northwestern Iran, where, during eight years, he fought the Seljuq sultans in Anatolia. In the Middle East during this period, three great powers confronted each other: Iran of the pagan Mongol khans, later converted to Islam, Turkey of the Muslim Ottoman princes, and Egypt of the Mamluk sultans.

Encouraged by his great victories, Hulagu resumed his march of conquest toward Syria and entered Damascus in 1259 after having conquered Aleppo. In the Battle of Ain Jalut, fought in 1260 in Palestine, the Mongol army was annihilated by the Mamluk troops, commanded by the Berber Turks. But the conflict between the Mongol power and Egypt would last several decades, well after the conversion of the khans to Islam. Meanwhile, Egypt, taking the place of a weakened Iraq, became the center of Islamic power and succeeded in repressing the Mongols and the Crusaders.

After the death in 1193 of Saladin (Salah al-Din al-Ayyubi), founder of the Ayyubid dynasty, the kingdom was divided. His successor al Malik al-'Adil inflicted a stinging defeat on the army of the Fourth Crusade, but afterwards Egypt was forced to co-exist with the Franks. A period of turmoil followed the assassination in 1250 of the last descendent of Saladin, the Sultan Turan Shah. The Mamluk 'Izz al-Din Aybeg married his widow and founded a Mamluk state in Egypt and Syria.

After his victory over the Mongols, and profiting from the chaos, the Mamluk

Timur-i Lang.
Timur-i Lang (Tamerlane), ruler of Mongol fiefs in Central Asia, invaded and annexed Iran in 1380. He then crossed into Iraq and ravaged Syria. It wasn't until his death in 1405 that the devastating invasions of the peoples of the steppe ended and the immense Mongol empire disintegrated.

Left: *Women in a mosque in Isfahan, Iran.*

Below: *Tamerlane in a Persian miniature.*

Figure with a flower. Miniature, School of Herat (1260). Topkapi Saray Museum, Istanbul.

General Baybars proclaimed himself Sultan of Egypt and Syria. By welcoming an 'Abbasid who escaped from the Mongols, he re-established the Sunni caliphate at Cairo, but it was an illusory caliphate, without real power.

In Anatolia, at the beginning of the fourteenth century, an Ottoman principality was created inside Byzantine Bithynia and took the name of its founder, 'Uthman. Thus began incessant frontier war with the Byzantines. Meanwhile, Ottoman troops crossed the Dardanelles in 1354 and penetrated into Europe through Macedonia, Bulgaria and Serbia.

Bayazid I, (Bajazet) (1389–1403), the fourth succesor of 'Uthman, was an ambitious commander and was not content with the vast kingdom he had inherited in Europe and Asia. He wanted to annex the Turkish Emirates as well, in order to unify all of Anatolia under his sole authority. But he was decisively defeated at the Battle of Ankara in 1402. In 1413, after a long period of civil wars, Muhammad I, a son of Bayazid, was able to reign uninterruptedly over an Ottoman state, even though it was shaken by several rebellions. The policy of territorial expansion resumed under Murad II (1421–1444).

Muhammad II, son of Murad, called *Fatih* (the Conqueror), rose to the throne in

Baybars. The Sunni state of Mamluks, instituted by Baybars, was founded on a complex dual military and civil administrative structure, in which civil servants were subordinate to the Mamluks. The hereditary transmission of the sultanate, which continued until 1383, was finally ended by rivalries between military factions that sought the throne. The conquest of Egypt by Ottoman Turks in 1517 put an end to the Mamluk dynasty and to the illusory power of the caliphate.

Murad II. This very energetic sultan, defender of Ottoman hegemony against the Hungarians in the Balkans, extended his power to Anatolia. He strengthened the state and modernized the army, which began using firearms in 1422.

1451 and aspired to unify the European and Anatolian parts of the empire. In 1453, he conquered Constantinople, thereby putting an end to the Byzantine empire. The former Byzantine capital became the residence of the sultan and the spiritual heart of the Muslim world in Europe.

In 1481, under the Sultanate of Bayazid II, after a long period of peace, Egypt and the Ottoman empire entered into war for the control of Cilicia. The conflict lasted from 1485 to 1490. Although the Ottomans were unable to gain a decisive victory, the war was proving to be a drain on Egypt. In addition, the Ottomans had to divert their attention and energies to Iran, the third largest Islamic power. In Azerbaijan in 1501, Shah Ishmael, ruler of the Turkomans, founded the Safavids, a new ambitious dynasty. After conquering Persia and Mesopotamia, he unified the country under a theocratic regime inspired by Shi'i doctrines and founded his capital in a region close to Ottoman territories. This victory impelled the Ottomans to annex Arabic-speaking lands from the south of the peninsula to the banks of the Persian gulf.

In 1517, the Ottoman sultan, Selim, received the keys of the Ka'bah and the title of caliph, thus legitimizing his protectorate over the Holy Places. The circumstances were favorable for a decisive attack against the shaky Mamluk state.

Shah 'Abbas I and his wife. Painting, School of Herat. Musée du Louvre, Paris.

Below, right and left: *Details of a miniature, School of Herat (1262). Topkapi Saray Museum, Istanbul.*

Fatih.
The first Ottoman legal codes are attributed to Fatih. He re-established the Janissary body and reorganized fiscal policy. His reign witnessed an intense period of urban construction.

Safavids and Ottomans. In 1511, the Safavids stirred up a revolt against the Ottomans in central Anatolia. Sultan Selim I the Cruel, who succeeded his elderly father in 1512, brought a bloody end to the revolt, exacerbating the political and religious conflict with the Persian Safavid dynasty. In 1514, the Safavid Ishmael declared war against the Ottomans, but the Iranian army was defeated by the Janissaries and the Ottoman artillery, allowing Selim I to seize the capital city of Tabriz.

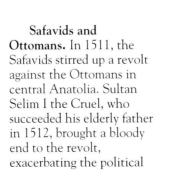

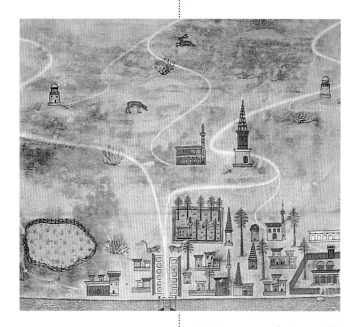

Place of pilgrimage. Turkish miniature (16th century). Page from a Manazilnam manuscript, The Itinerary, *which celebrated the first Persian expedition of Sulayman the Magnificent. Topkapi Saray Museum, Istanbul.*

In 1520, the accession of the Sultan Sulayman, called the Magnificent, marked the apogee of the Ottoman empire. Reforms were instituted at every level of political and social organization. Turkey made its debut on the European stage, and after the victory of 1526 over Hungary, the Turks arrived at the gates of Vienna. This was the high water mark of Turkish expansion into Europe. With Sulayman's death in 1566, the power passed into the hands of the Grand Wazirs. Their iniquitous management of land, taxation and administrative systems provoked endemic rebellions. In 1683, a second siege of Vienna ended with a resounding Turkish defeat, and this was followed by other important military defeats and the loss of numerous provinces. The Ottoman empire became the "sick man," whose weakness threatened European stability.

Meanwhile, Shah 'Abbas, who had risen to the Iranian throne in 1588, presided over an era of peace and prosperity. The army was reorganized, Shi'a became the religion of the state, and the establishment of new relations with Europe opened commercial markets.

With the death of 'Abbas in 1629, the Safavid dynasty went into an irrevocable decline. Despite the success of Nadir, a talented military commander, the relations between the Islamic states and their European antagonists were not fundamentally altered.

The crisis of the Ottoman empire. The Ottoman defeat at Vienna and the disadvantageous conditions in the Treaty of Karlowitz of 1699 marked the beginning of a weakening of the forces of Islam before the expansionist policies of Europe. The Russian army and the nations of western Europe began to threaten and conquer Muslim territories. The balance of power had changed on a military and commercial level, and this affected all of the Muslim countries.

The apogee of the Safavid era. It was under the reign of Shah 'Abbas (1588–1629) that architecture and painting reached their peak, notably in the miniatures from the school of Rida 'Abbasi.

Conflicts with the Russians and the signature of several disadvantageous, even humiliating, peace treaties confirmed the decline of Ottoman power in the Middle East. Russia also threatened Iran, which attempted to reconquer the regions of Caucasia that it had been forced to cede to the Tsar. This offensive was guided by Aga Muhammad, a leader of the Turkomans, who seized northern Persia and made Teheran his capital in 1785. Crowned shah in 1794, Aga Muhammad founded the Qajar dynasty. His successors attempted to govern by opposing Russia's expansionist designs on Caucasia and England's on Afghanistan. In 1828, Russia imposed a peace treaty that was humiliating for Iran, joined forces with the Greeks, and declared war against Turkey. What had been a territorial struggle evolved into a frontal attack on Islam. In Asia, the Russians advanced towards the south, while in the west, centuries after the *reconquista*, the Spanish and Portuguese campaigned in Africa.

Islam and Europe

The contribution of Islam to the development of European civilization, whether directly or through the mediation of Mediterranean cultures, is very important. Following the Crusades, the social, economic and cultural exchanges between the two worlds increased, but the enormous differences dividing them often led to military solutions.

Isfahan, the royal mosque (16th century) constructed by Shah 'Abbas the Great.

Nadir. Head of a Turkoman tribe in the service of the Safavids, this talented commander headed the counterattack against the Iranians and gained the governance of western Persia. At the death of the shah in 1736, he acceded to the throne.

Abraham Pacha (1718–1730) Great Wazir of the Sultan Ahmad III, he founded a policy of openness to the West and of improvement of political relations. He oversaw the introduction of the printing press into the Ottoman world and presided over administrative and financial reforms.

Tombs of Mamluks, Cairo (1564). Originally enslaved soldiers, the Mamluks governed Egypt for three centuries. They were excellent warriors and great defenders of Islam.

In 1798, French troops, led by Bonaparte, arrived in Egypt. This was the first significant offensive launched by modern Europe against the Islamic world. Although it was a military operation, it was also the first scientific exploration of the area. In addition, it exposed the traditional world of Islam to modern European political ideas. The French occupation of Egypt was of short duration. Muslim control was re-established thanks to the intervention of England, while the expeditionary corps led by Muhammad 'Ali contributed to the French defeat in 1801. Subsequently made governor of Egypt, Muhammad 'Ali undertook important military, land, and fiscal reforms. In 1841, he was named hereditary viceroy, and Egypt obtained complete independence from the Ottoman empire.

Meanwhile, an event that would have major social, political, and religious consequences was taking place in the Arabian peninsula. Muhammad ibn 'Abd al-Wahhab allied with Muhammad ibn Sa'ud, the head of a tribe from the Najd region of central Arabia, in order to impose his religious doctrines by force. The rigid Sunni reform movement of Wahhabiyyah, founded in 1746, was a reformulation of the most ancient doctrines of the Hanbali legal schools and the theories of Ibn Taymiyyah. Al-Wahhab's thoughts inspired an entire movement of Islamic modernism; its influence continued long after its initial success. The Wahhabis conquered Medina in 1804

Muhammad 'Ali. This great reformer introduced a modern educational system, created universities of medicine, engineering, and chemistry. The adoption of European technology contributed to industrial development. In 1821, at Bulaq, in Cairo, the first printing press of the Egyptian state was founded, with the first Arab newspaper appearing in 1828. Even though it was used solely for printing an official governmental gazette, the press marks the institutional return of the Arabic language. With the construction of railroads and the opening of the Suez Canal in 1869, Egypt regained a strategic role in world affairs.

and Mecca in 1806, thus gaining control of an important part of Arabia's territories. But in 1811, at the request of the Ottoman sultan, the governor of Egypt, Muhammad 'Ali, mounted an expedition against the Wahhabis.

In 1830, the colonization of North Africa began with French annexation of Algeria, which, while nominally under Ottoman rule, was, in fact, self-governing. In 1832, the Emir 'Abd al-Qadir, a Sufi philosopher and poet, led the Algerian War of Independence against France. The rebellion was defeated in 1847, and 'Abd al-Qadir was forced into exile. In Tunisia, advisory committees were formed to take steps toward a new Arab unity. They were interrupted in 1881 by the French occupation. Other countries in North Africa were colonized by the Europeans. The Turks handed Libya over to the Italians in 1911, but Italian rule came to an end in 1922. In Morocco, the reign of the Sultan 'Abd al-'Aziz, begun in 1894, ended in 1912. The country became a French protectorate with Marshal Lyautey as resident-general.

In Turkey, the Sultan Ma'mud II (1808–1839) launched a program of reforms. His reorganization of the army and the state was directly inspired by the French model. In 1865, the Young Turks movement was formed, founded on a blend of patriotism, Ottoman constitutionalism and Islamic modernism. The constitutional movement developed until the promulgation of the constitution by Sultan 'Abd al-Hamid II.

The insurrection of 1908, followed by elections, brought the Young Turks a parliamentary majority, then to power by a coup in 1913. The following year saw the end of their attempt at democracy. Turkey became involved in the First World War in alliance with the Central Powers.

A minaret in the center of Marrakech, Morocco. The town was founded in 1077 by the Almoravids, who came from the south by the caravan routes from Sudan. Marrakech has been an important center of Islamic theological study ever since.

The Constitutions. The promulgation of the Constitution of 1861 by the Bey of Tunis, introduced a constitutional regime for the first time to an Islamic country, but it was revoked soon afterwards in 1864. Likewise, in Egypt the governor turned over questions of agriculture, education and taxes to a parliamentary assembly. These institutional reforms, however, did not slow the decline of Islamic countries facing bankruptcy, disorder, military interventions and foreign occupation. Throughout the Arab world, the emergence of ideological nationalist and Islamic movements prefigured the cultural renaissance and the re-establishment of political independence.

The town of Jenin in a painting by David Roberts (1839). The 19th century was characterized by wars of resistance against colonization and by cultural revival in the context of a return to religious sources.

Below right: *Cairo at twilight.*

In Egypt, a Persian religious thinker and reformer, Jamal al-Din al-Afghani, championed modernist Islamic ideas that nourished nationalist aspirations. He was the founder of the Jami'ah al-Islamiyya religious movement. His principal Egyptian disciple, Sheik Muhammad Abdou, would perpetuate his ideas. Named Grand Mufti of Egypt in 1899, he supported liberal reforms within influential circles of the movement of Islamic modernism.

In 1870 in Sudan, the danger of a new bitter schism emerged, when Muhammad Ahmad ibn 'Abd Allah, who presented himself as the incarnation of Mahdi, the twelfth Shi'i imam, founded an Islamic fundamentalist movement. In 1881, a rebellion of officers, supported by the constitutionalists and the followers of al-Afghani, provoked England's occupation of Egypt. The Mahdi called for a holy war against the Egyptian regime in Sudan. His military success gave him control over the eastern part of the country. It was not until 1898 that the Anglo-Egyptian troops, commanded by Lord Kitchener, succeeded in conquering the Mahdi's army. But his undeniably popular following is still alive today.

The liberal ideas of the commercial Christian bourgeoisie were influential in Beirut and enhanced the efforts towards Islamic modernization. In 1866 Protestant missionaries created the American University of Beirut. Attracting intellectuals from throughout Syria, it contributed considerably to a renaissance of Arab thought and culture. In 1912 in Beirut, a committee of reform against the risk of Turkish cultural domination was born. It tried to have the Ottoman state recognize Arabic as the official language. Another committee, called *al-Arabiyya al-Fatat*, instituted in Paris in 1911 and strongly

Salafiyya. In Cairo in 1898, Muhammad 'Abduh and his disciple Rashid Rida founded the weekly, al-Manar, which they used as a vehicle to diffuse their policy of reform, based on a return to the values of the *salaf*, the founders of Islam.

represented in Beirut in 1913, demanded complete liberation from Ottoman domination.

In Arabia, the Wahhabiyyah doctrines received the support of the Saudi dynasty, who, thanks to an alliance with England against the Turks, had extended its power over a large part of western Arabia at the beginning of the First World War. Immediately following the war, the head of the Saudi dynasty, 'Abd al-'Aziz ibn Sa'ud, imposed his authority over the new territories of North and South Arabia. In 1932 the kingdom of Saudi Arabia was proclaimed.

In 1919, in Turkey, a young officer named Mustafa Kemal, later called Ataturk, the Father of Turks, organized the nationalist resistance against the Allies in the center of Anatolia. Assuming power, Kemal proclaimed Turkey a republic and abolished the sultanate. At the same time, Islam ceased to be the state religion, and the Latin alphabet replaced the Arab alphabet.

In 1906, in Iran, the constitutional revolution obliged the shah to convoke a national assembly and promulgate a constitution; then civil war forced him to flee to Russia for refuge in 1908. In 1909, under the reign of Ahmad Shah, the creation of the Anglo-Iranian Oil Company introduced the system of concessions for the exploitation of the oil resources of Persia. It was the

Saudis in prayer at Abu Dhabi, United Arab Emirates. On the international scene, the Gulf countries and Saudi Arabia maintain a balance between mysticism and obscurantism, morally virtuous and, at the same time, retrograde.

Naqshbandi and Wahhabis. From the 18th century, these two religious movements opposed threats from the West and the decadence of the Islamic civilization. Originating in India, of Sufi inspiration, the Naqshbandi order was introduced in the fourteenth century into the countries of the Middle East and Turkey. In Egypt, spiritual reforms, stimulated by scholars and Naqshbandi masters were suppressed by the French invaders. This resulted in a battle for liberation. The Wahhabiyyah movement, though distanced from Sufi mysticism, also advocated a reform of Islam. Even though the Saudi Wahhabi dynasty lost power following the Egyptian intervention of 1818, the inspirational ideas of the movement are still alive today.

Interior of the Mosque of Khumayni at Teheran (Iran). The Khumayni revolution (1979) provoked a strenghtening of Islam and encouraged the birth of new Islamic states.

beginning of a new era in the relations between the Islamic countries and the European powers. The same year, the agreement between Iran and England guaranteed the independence and integrity of Iranian territory. This, however, did not prevent the occupation of a large part of the country by Russian and English troops during the First World War. In 1921, an officer by the name of Reza Khan Sawadkuhi seized power. His dictatorship was strengthened in 1925, when he overthrew the Qajar dynasty of shahs. He proclaimed himself shah and founded the Pahlavi dynasty.

The Independent states

The upheavals resulting from the First World War thus resulted in the weakening of Islamic forces under the pressure of Western powers. The division of Arab territories between the victors involved the creation of new states, whose borders were completely

redefined and whose administration was subject to the European powers and mandated by the League of Nations.

Mesopotamia, which became a monarchy under the British mandate, was called "Iraq", from an ancient Arab name. The southern part of Syria entrusted to the English, took the name of Palestine, while the north, ceded to France, gave birth after several modifications to the Republics of Syria and Lebanon. With the Balfour

The Pahlavi. Riza Shah undertook a policy of modernization and centralization of power in Iran. His son, Muhammad Reza, who continued the work of his father, was ousted by the Islamic revolution of Khumayni in 1979.

The Arabs and Israel. In 1947, after long and dramatic debates, the General Assembly of the United Nations adopted the resolution which ratified the division of Palestine and led to the proclamation of the state of Israel on May 14, 1948.

The first Israeli-Arab war inaugurated a long series of conflicts between Israel and the Arab Independent States, concluding in unstable alliances. Military attempts to oppose the state of Israel led to divisions between Arab countries and profoundly disrupted

Declaration in 1917, the English began to support the creation of a Jewish homeland within the framework of the territorial limits decided on by the League of Nations.

Between the two wars, the only states of the Middle East who succeeded in conserving their independence and enjoying complete sovereignty were Turkey, Iran and Afghanistan. Saudi Arabia and Yemen also gained their independence, but in Egypt and Iraq, independence was mainly of a formal nature. In the decades that followed, these regimes obtained complete political autonomy. After expelling the French, Syria and Lebanon added themselves to the list of independent countries and entered the League of Arab States, which was proclaimed in March 1945. The incorporation of Jordan into the League took place the following year. The list of independent countries grew longer: Libya (1951), Sudan (1956), Tunisia, Morocco and Mauritania (1960), Kuwait (1961), Algeria (1962, after a long and bloody war of liberation), and the United Arab Emirates (1971).

Jerusalem: In the foreground, the Mosque of the Rock.

Below: *Iraqi child.*

the entire region. The years immediately following the war saw revolts and bloody coups directed against the regimes that were considered responsible, in league with the Western forces, for a defeat that allowed the growth of the Jewish state and the introduction of this "foreign body" in the heart of the Arab world. Although Israel has now obtained the recognition of the Arab countries, the question of the Palestinian nation still remains an obstacle to peace in the region.

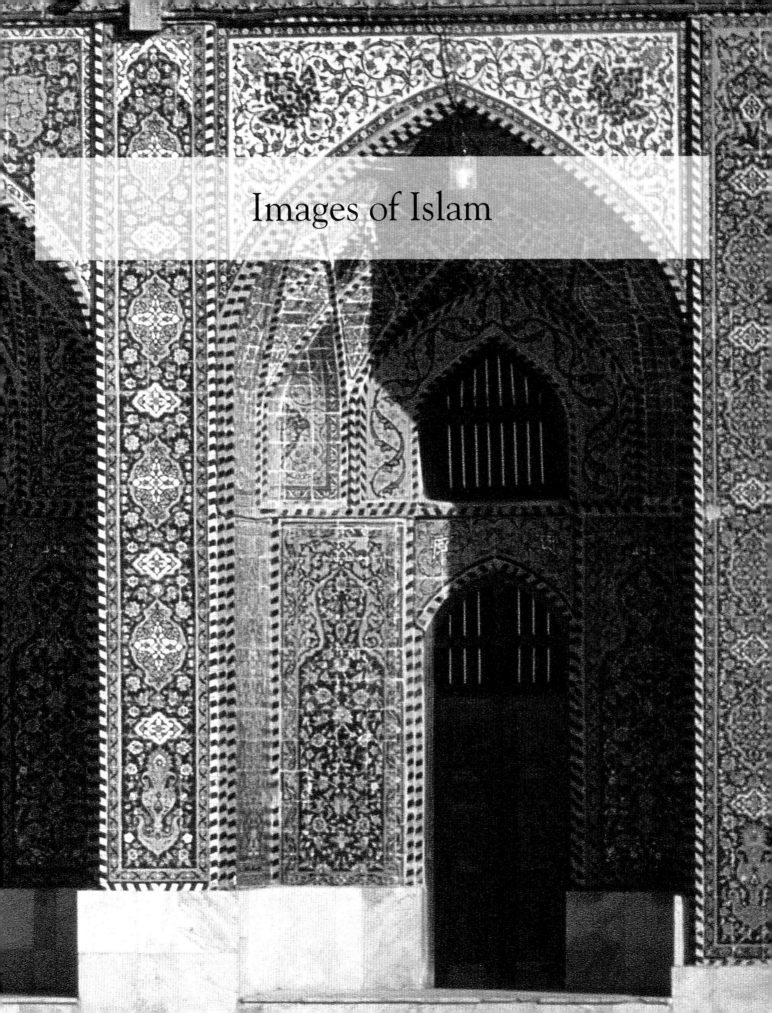

Images of Islam

Preceding spread: *View of the Mausoleum of Karbala, the holy city of the Shi'a, in Iraq.*

The sacred rock inside the Dome of the Rock at Jerusalem.

Right hand page: *The faithful in prayer on the esplanade in front of the Dome. The construction of the building under the Umayyad Caliph Abd al-Malik ibn Marwan, started in 687 and was completed in*

692. The sacred rock, which is located today inside the large polygonal building, is an object of veneration for Muslims, Jews, and Christians. Muslims believe that it is on this rock that the Prophet began his ascension and that the Dome of the Rock was constructed at the summit of the ancient

Mount Moriah. It was here that Ishmael, whom the Arabs consider their progenitor, was to have been sacrificed. The Aqsa Mosque is located near the Dome of the Rock.

A corner of the courtyard of the Great Mosque of Ziyadatr Allah in Kairouan, Tunisia. Constructed in several stages between 836 and 875, it was always among Islam's most important centers of study and prayer.

*The minaret of the Great
Mosque of Ziyadatr Allah in
Kairouan, Tunisia. The
juxtaposition of Western and
Eastern motifs can be seen in
the decoration of the mosque.*

Below and right hand page:
*Details of decorations in
ceramic in the Great Mosque.*

The Great Mosque of al-Mutawakkil, in Samarra, Iraq, constructed between 848 and 852. The surrounding walls, now in ruins, demarcate an esplanade, famous as the largest enclosed space in the Islamic world. At the left, the malwiyya, *a spiral minaret fifty-five meters in height, was* constructed following the Mesopotamian tradition of a tower with a spiral staircase, derived from the Babylonian ziggurat.

Right hand page: *The minaret of the Mosque of Abu Dulaf, near the Great Mosque in Samarra, is the same shape as* the malwiyya *but is smaller and more slender. Samarra, 150 kilometers to the north of Baghdad, underwent rapid expansion when the colossal army of Turkish slaves, 70,000 men, was garrisoned here under the caliphates of al-Mu'tasim (833–847) and al-Mutawakkil (847–861).*

The colonnade of the Great Mosque of Córdoba and its West Gate. The mosque was constructed in only one year (786–787) by the Umayyad Caliph Abd al-Rahman, who made Córdoba his capital. Representing one of the masterpieces of classical Islamic architecture, the stone building was originally composed of one prayer room and eleven naves set perpendicular to the qibla wall (wall facing the direction of Mecca). The sahn (courtyard) was connected by a door to the prayer room. In 951, Abd al-Rahman III enlarged the sahn towards the south and constructed a new minaret. This construction was completed in 962 by al-Hakam II.

The Friday Mosque at Isfahan, Iran. Under Alp Arslan (1063–1072), Isfahan became the capital of the Seljuk empire. The town was centered around the square area in front the Great Mosque's portal, constructed at the end of the ninth century, with some later additions or reconstructions.

Right and left hand pages:
Two images of the interior of the Friday Mosque, at Isfahan, Iran. The mosque was rebuilt during the Mongol era (fourteenth century).

The minbar *on which the imam sat for Friday prayer. Within the mosque, the imam does not have a hierarchical or authoritative position. He may be its guardian and can lead the prayer, but in his absence any believer can assume this function.*

The portico of los Arrayanes, and to the right, the portico of los Leones and the room of los Reyes of the Alhambra of Granada. It was Muhammad I, called Ibn al-Ahmar (1230–1272) who founded the Kingdom of Grenada and constructed the citadel of the Alhambra, the pink fortress that became his capital. The dimensions, the splendor of decoration, the use of ornamental pools — all converge to present a perfect image of the Qur'anic paradise.

Following spread:
The ornamentation of the room of las Dos Hermanas.

Persian plate from the thirteenth century decorated with nobles and horsemen. Benaki Museum, Athens.

Right hand page: Persian carpet depicting animal scenes. Museo Poldi Pezzoli, Milan. Figurative art played a very important role in Islamic culture: there are no passages in the Qur'an that forbid figurative works, although idols and their adoration are condemned. Reality can be represented, but man must not try to compete with God as creator.

Glass perfume flagon with decorations in enamel. Egypt or Syria, thirteenth century. Museo civico di arte medievale, Bologna.

Right, above: *Ivory chest painted with lions. Museo del Bargello, Florence.*

Right below: *Mosque lamp in enameled glass. Syria, fourteenth century. Museo del Bargello, Florence.*

Right hand page: *Bronze and silver vase. Second half of the thirteenth century. North Africa (Morocco or Egypt). Museo del Bargello, Florence.*

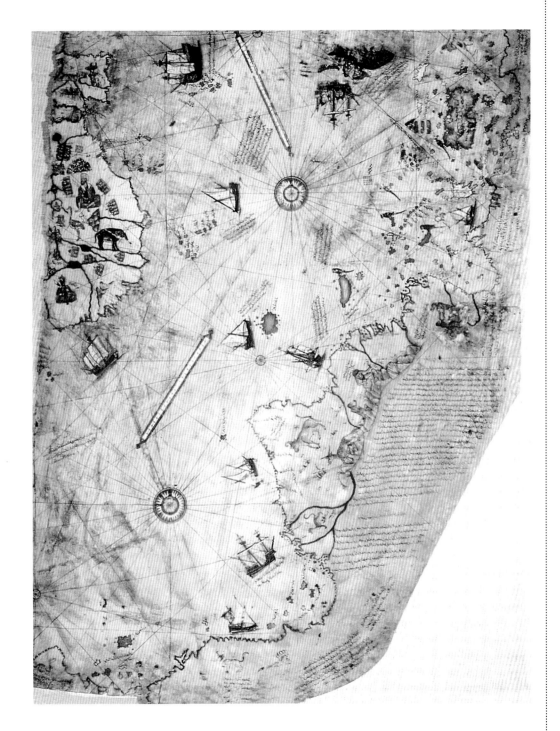

Fragment of Admiral Piri Rei's (1513) world map, depicting the Atlantic Ocean and the coasts of the Iberian Peninsula, West Africa, and South America. Naval Museum, Istanbul. The Turkish admiral drew his own map of the world, basing it on the map drawn by Christopher Columbus as well as on Portuguese, Alexandrian and Arab maps.

Left hand page:
Page from the manuscript of Abu Ma'chat (Cairo, circa 1250) with a miniature representing astrological figures. Conjunction of the moon and Jupiter in Sagittarius. Bibliothèque nationale, Paris. European astrology and astronomy were strongly influenced by Islamic science, as can be witnessed by the fame of Abu Ma'chat and the great number of technical terms derived from Arabic.

Following spread:
At Jiddah, the pilgrims prepare themselves to enter into the holy sanctuary of Mecca.

*Timimun, in the Algerian
desert. An immense crowd
assembles to celebrate the birth
of the Prophet. Each Islamic
country commemorates this
birthday according to its own
traditions. For all believers, it is
a holiday dedicated to prayer
and spirituality.*

Gathering for the end of Ramadan in the streets of Cairo, in front of the Mosque of Mohan Disin. With the end of the month of Ramadan and of the fast (sawm), *the Muslim world celebrates the triumph of the faith and their victory over evil and temptation. In jubilation, the faithful exchange wishes of peace for themselves and for the rest of the world.*

*Views of the Qait Bey, Cairo.
This building was constructed
under the Mamluk Sultan Qait
Bey. It is composed of a tomb,
shown here, and a* madrassah,
(school of Islamic learning).

Woman in prayer in a cemetery in Istanbul. Muslim cemeteries are usually very quiet. People visit regularly to recite the Surah Fatihah, (the Prologue) for the deceased, as well as several other surah of the Qur'an.

Right hand page:
An imam prays in the Eyub Mosque, Istanbul. The mosque is the ideal location for prayer, meditation, and repetition of the name of Allah. But the mosque also serves as a meeting place for the community; in the sahn, theological lessons are given, and the Qur'an is studied.

Above: *Interior of a mosque at Miri in Malaysia.*

Below: *Prayer in a mosque in Kuala Lumpur, Malaysia.*

Right hand page, above: *Young students of a Qur'anic school with their professor, at Miri.*

Right hand page, below: *A moment of reflection and study in a mosque. There are currently several hundred million Muslims in Asia.*

96

Students of a Qur'anic school in the Sultanate of Oman. Qur'anic schools have played an essential role in the preservation of the Arabic language. During periods of decline, the teaching of the Qur'an permitted young Muslims to maintain a bond with their culture and religion.

Right hand page:
The ancient town of San'a' in Yemen, has preserved the characteristics of Arab architecture from the pre-Islamic period until today.

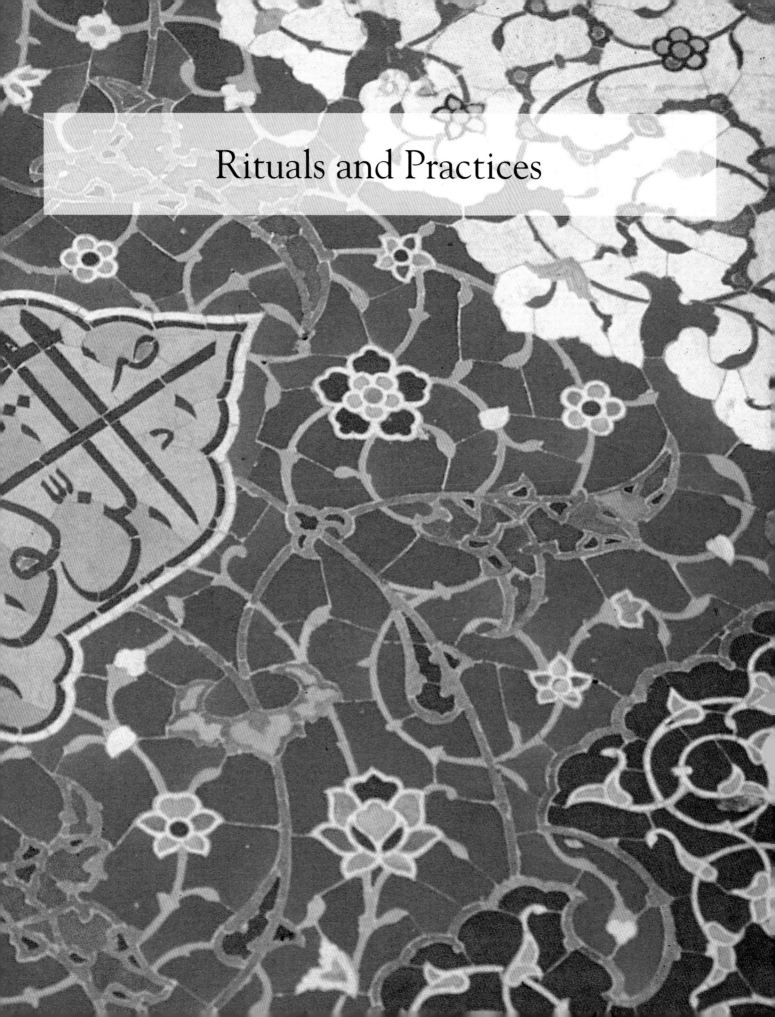

Rituals and Practices

Calligraphy of a verse of the Qur'an in thuluth yali *style by Yussuf Dhanun (1976). The Iraqi Cultural Centre, London. Arabic is the language of the Qur'an, and the faithful must know at least the essential Qur'anic verses in the sacred language.*

Below: *Reading of the Qur'an in a mosque in Cairo. It was only during the last few years of Muhammad's life that he dictated the Qur'an to his Companions. Until then, it had been orally transmitted.*

Preceding spread:
Detail of the mosaic decoration of the Mosque of the Imam, Isfahan, Iran.

The Qur'an is the supreme witness of the Revelation, the Word of God, the archetypal holy text. The revelation that was made to the Prophet while he had retreated for meditation in a cave on Mount Hira, near Mecca, is not only the collection of divine messages addressed to man; equally important, it governs the everyday life of the Muslim.

The word Qur'an signifies recitation or reading, in Arabic. Arabic is the language in which the Revelation is written, but it is also considered by Muslims as inextricably bound up with Revelation. The tone, inflection, and melody of Arabic cannot be separated from its liturgical role in the Revelation, making Arabic the sacred language of Islam.

Clearly the Qur'an does not speak exclusively to Arabs. However, the incantatory texts voiced during the prayers, along with the verses from the Quran, which are the foundation of the religion, must be learned and recited in Arabic, the only language which does not distort its message.

The Qur'an, living root of metaphysical and religious knowledge, finds in this archaic language an unequaled suggestive power. It is the masterpiece of Arab literature: "I call to witness the lucent Book, / That We made it a distinctly lucid Qur'an that you may understand. / It is inscribed in the original Book (of Books) with Us, sublime, dispenser of (all) laws," (Qur'an 43: 2-4).

The Qur'an is the manifestation of the unique voice of God, the third revelation after the Jewish Torah and the Christian Gospel. For this reason, the believers of these three religions are called *ahl al-kitab*, People of the Book or of the Revelation.

During the Prophet's life, and for a short time following his death, the safeguarding of the Qur'an was entrusted entirely to the memory of the faithful who recited the prayers, and to the memorization of those who were called Living Receptacles of the Qur'an. It was only in the last years of his life that Muhammad undertook the dictation of the Revelation to his "secretary" Companions, a fragile account which has survived in spite of time, textual additions, and substitutions of apocryphal writings for the original. The first caliph, Abu Bakr, is responsible for initiating the recension of the Qur'an. It was only after the commotion caused by the apostasies following the death of the Prophet (wars of conquest which took the lives of numerous of his Companions and the fight against false prophets) that people began to fear the loss of the Holy Book. Therefore, the second caliph, 'Umar, along with Zayd ibn Tabet, the Prophet's secretary and scribe, established a more thorough collection, of which Umar had several copies made. Finally, 'Uthman, the third caliph, ordered an official edition

Arabic - the language of the Revelation.
The sacred nature of the Arabic language is emphasized in the Qur'an: "And this (Qur'an) is a revelation from the Lord of all the worlds / Which the trusted spirit descended with / To (communicate) to your heart that you may be a warner / In eloquent Arabic. / This is (indicated) in the Books of earlier people." (Qur'an 26: 192-196).

The Qur'an is responsible for the spread of the Arabic language. It was through this Book that Arabic became the common language of Muslims and has endured until today. Although its syntax and lexicon have been clarified and codified over time, the Qur'an remains the masterpiece of the Arabic language. Islam considers its expressive power miraculous. Its pre-

founded on Zayd's text. At the same time, he ordered all other versions destroyed, indicating the importance of this edition.

The Qur'an does not follow the chronological order of the revelations. The chapters are ordered according to length (in most cases), with the exception of the first chapter. The Qur'an is divided into 114 *surah*, or chapters, and each *surah* is divided into *ayat*, or verses. (In the citations of the Qur'an in this book, the first number indicates the *surah*; the second, the *ayat*.) The second *surah* is composed of 286 verses and the last contain three to six. The Qur'an contains a little more than six thousand *ayat*, of unequal length. In their writing, as in their reading, all but a few *surah* are preceded by the formula, *Bismillah ar-Rahman ar-Raheem* (In the name of Allah, most benevolent, ever-merciful), which later became the opening formula of all Muslim writings and religious rites. Its recitation can precede any act that the Muslim performs. The opening *surah* of the Qur'an, called Fatihah, the Prologue, is a brief prayer emphasizing Allah's primordial role in the religion, as well as in life of the Muslim.

The first *surah*, which were revealed in Mecca, are called the *makkiyat*, Meccans; they are shorter than those revealed in Medina, which are called *madanayaht*, Medinans. Addressing the rules of public organization, the Medinans contain directions on how to organize and lead the new *umma* (community).

The Qur'an addresses both moral and religious subjects as well as the social organization of the new state. Meditations on the destiny of man are intertwined with laws concerning the establishment of an Islamic community. The range of concerns is broad, but the chief concern remains the betterment of human beings. God Himself governs human activity, as long as it is directed toward the search for perfection. The ideal of justice originates from the supremacy of the moral law, which man can neither make nor break according to his will, since God is its foundation. Within the religious message of the holy text we find a theory of the nature of reality, a collection of moral and legal instructions which constitute the basis of the Law, a theology, and a cosmology. At the center is the concept of God, as creator and lord of the universe, whose attributes of power and mercy cannot be separated; rather, they necessarily intermingle in their unity.

The Qur'an underlines the importance of prayer, encourages fasting, imposes the *zakat* (the almsgiving

Manuscript of the Qur'an in Kufic characters on parchment (7th century). Museum of Turco-Islamic Art, Istanbul.

Below: *Calligraphy of a Qur'anic verse in* diwani *style by Yussuf Dhanun (1981). The Iraqi Cultural Centre, London.*

eminent role in the history of Arab literature does not only hold for the time of its origin, but remains true today. The *i'jaz* (the inimitable character of the Qur'an) is a dogma claimed by all schools who study the message and the style of the Book.

Stylized Turkish writing. Wooden table (14th century). Museum of Turco-Islamic Art.

tithe), and stipulates that a pilgrimage must be made to Mecca at least once in a Muslim's life.

It also calls for the *jihad*, a complex concept which means "call to war" only in certain cases. In general, *jihad* means the striving for perfection on the path of God by the giving of one's self and of one's worldly goods. This notion of an all-encompassing effort applies to prayer, to the *zakat*, to the energy with which one desires good and abhors evil, toward the goal of the expansion of Islam, and, by extension, to war — which can only be declared in particular circumstances.

In several places the Qur'an prohibits *riba*, (usury), *maysir*, (gambling), and the consumption of alcohol: "Satan only wishes to create among you enmity and hatred through wine and gambling..." (Qur'an 5: 91). It is also forbidden to eat carrion, blood or pork. "You tell them: 'In all of the commands revealed to me I find nothing which men have been forbidden to eat except carrion and running blood and flesh of the swine for it is unclean, or meat consecrated in the name of some other than God, which is profane,'" (Qur'an 6: 145).

The Qur'an is, above all, a book of principles and of religious and moral admonition. Nevertheless, it gives fundamental legal directives on questions of slavery, the condition of women, marriage, family, and rules of inheritance.

It holds that women and their children should remain under a man's guardianship. The Qur'an proposes a better life for women than that of the pre-Islamic period. Spouses complement each other. "They (your wives) are your dress as you are theirs." (Qur'an 2: 187). Women enjoy the same rights as men, even if men benefit from a privileged status.

Polygamy proved to be a solid foundation for the family as long as it was regulated by law. The generations which followed the death of the Prophet were careful in interpreting the sacred text. However, because of the rapid extension of the Islamic state and the subsequent diversification of its ethnic and cultural composition, numerous commentaries were required. These commentaries also were written in response to controversies that ignited movements that demanded a return to Islam's origins, to tradition, and to the people and circumstances of the Revelation. This led to the writing of the *Jami 'al-bayanfi tafsir al-Qur'an* (The Full Exposition of Qur'anic Commentary). This work by Tabari (839–923), which is the

An immense narration. The Qur'an is didactic and historical. It tells the history of peoples, tribes, kings, prophets, and saints. It speaks of the Biblical adventures of Noah, Abraham, Joseph and Moses, the story of the birth and childhood of Jesus, and post-Biblical episodes; and it relays the treasures of colloquial Arab wisdom. It conveys a universal message.

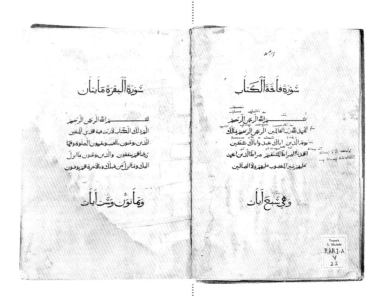

most important commentary on the Qur'an, is founded on testimonies from the first generation of Muslims. Other commentaries of Sufi inspiration had a more esoteric aim. The commentaries on the Qur'an permitted new questions to be posed and new responses to be made.

According to the great theologian Ibn al-Qayym (d. 1350), the giving of the revelation followed a hierarchical order. At times, the Archangel Gabriel united with the Prophet and poured the revelation directly into his heart: "And this (Qur'an) is a revelation from the Lord of all the worlds, which the trusted spirit descended with to (communicate) to your heart that you may be a warner in eloquent Arabic" (Qur'an 26 : 192-195). At other times, Gabriel would present himself to Muhammad in his angelic form to dictate the verses to him. The instances where the Prophet, in a state resembling ecstasy, received the word of God directly, were the most intense form of the revelations. The revelation was thus a dramatic occurrence, an event which was not only spiritual but also physical. It could manifest itself by sounds of bells, by whistling, or by violent fevers which made Muhammad lose consciousness and left him soaked in sweat.

The force and intensity of the revelation is described in the Qur'an. "If We had sent down this Qur'an to a mountain you would have seen it turn desolate and split into two for fear of God" (Qur'an 59: 21).

Qur'an printed in Venice in Arabic characters by Paganino and Alessandro Paganini (1537–1538). Biblioteca dei Frati Minori di San Michele in Isola, Venice.

Left: *Sunni Qur'anic school in Torbat-e Jam, Iran.*

Below: *Modern edition of the Qur'an.*

Qur'anic schools.
The teaching and the commentaries on the Qur'an were articulated and transmitted in inner courtyards, under arcades, or in any other circular space in a mosque. In both large cities and villages the Qur'anic schools, the *madrassah*, were often the only schools that existed. The children learned to read, write, and recite the Qur'an by heart. Even today, in small towns it is the Qur'anic school that provides elementary education.

Detail of a Turkish miniature (18th century). Museum of Turco-Islamic Art, Istanbul.

Below: *The name of Muhammad in a popular modern print. Episodes from the life of Muhammad are found in the* hadith, *and serve as examples for the lives of Muslims. The* sunnah *is the religious practice which stems from it.*

In addition to being the Messenger of God and archetypal interpreter of the Qur'an, during the course of his life the Prophet was the sole religious and political leader of the Muslims. His time on earth, his sufferings, his pains, his difficulties and his ordeals are found in the *a hadith* (the reports), which he passed on, and in the *sunnah*, which recount the events of his everyday life and offer guidance for Muslims' questions about their individual and collective lives.

After the deaths of the Prophet and his Companions, between the seventh and eighth centuries, the first theological assemblies appeared, and the *a hadith* began to be collected, which allowed for the development of the law.

For Muslims, the nature of Qur'anic authority is different and more significant than the authority of the Prophet, who was only its vehicle. The Qur'an urges all believers to obey the Messenger of God. It advocates imitation of the Prophet, whose religious and social conduct was a model for the individual Muslim, as it was for the entire Islamic community. Indeed, the Prophet himself made a clear distinction between his own sayings and those of the Qur'an.

Only in extraordinary situations must one must look to the Qur'an to confirm the Prophet's decisions. Following the Qur'an, the *a hadith* are the most important source of the *shari'ah* (the law), and of the *tariqah*, (the mystical path). This teaching, intended for all, is the model which regulates practical everyday life to the smallest detail and is the source that unites diverse peoples.

Hadith literally means narrative, story, or anecdote. A *hadith* is composed of a *matn* (text), and an *isnad* (the chain of transmitters), which gives the text credibility by listing the genealogy of those who transmitted it. The *hadith*, or verbal narration of a religious tradition, naturally directs one to the *sunnah*, which is the corresponding religious practice. The *sunnah* is called the non-verbal, silent, or living transmission. The word *sunnah* literally means way, footpath, diagram, or outline; but the term evolved to mean the behavior of the Prophet. The details of Islamic practices are defined in the *sunnah*. For example, if the Qur'an orders prayer and fasting, precise instructions on how to perform these requirements can be found in the example of the Prophet and in the instructions set out in the *sunnah*. The collection of *hadith* constitutes a fundamental part of the *sunnah* of the Prophet. The *hadith* were transmitted by several of Muhammad's Companions.

At the death of the last of these, the *Tabi'un*, the Successors or disciples, who had lived with the Companions and compiled the orally-transmitted *hadith*, continued the chain, transmitting the *hadith* to their disciples. Some *hadith* were written by the Companions on pages known as *sahifah*.

Following an inquiry which, in its initial stage, stretched over a period of three generations, near the middle of the ninth century, the corpus of *hadith* received its definitive form.

The corpus of the *a hadith* had to be established before the legal function of the *sunnah* could begin to

The *hadith* of 'A'isha. Muhammad was actively engaged in social life. He was married, raised his children, and remained friends with them. He was also a legislator, judge, and even warrior, when the case called for it. In a *hadith* attributed to 'A'isha, her response to the question, "In the home, what work did the Prophet do?" was, "He helped his family and when he heard the call to prayer, he went."

Obedience to the Prophet. "He who obeys the Apostle obeys God..." (Qur'an 4: 80) because, "... you certainly guide them to the right path, / The path of God..." (Qur'an 42: 52-53). The Qur'an contains numerous verses demanding obedience.

be applied. It was the jurist Muhammad ash-Shafi'i (767–820), founder of one of the four traditional Islamic schools of law, who imposed the regulated usage of the *sunnah* of the Prophet. He accorded the *sunnah* a degree of authority directly beneath that of the Qur'an.

Only five of the collections of *hadith* were unanimously decreed *sahih*, (authentic). The most important is the *Sahih* of Isma'il al-Bukhari (810–870). Others were compiled later: the *Sahih* of Abu-l-Husayn (816–875), the *Sonnan* of Abu Da'wd (d. 875), the *Sahih* of al-Tirmidhi (824–892), and the *Sonnan* of al-Nasa'i (d. 915). Other collections of *a hadith* include the *Sonnan* of Ibn Majah (d. 886), the *Muwatta'* of Malik ibn Anas (712–795), the *Musnad* of al-Darimah (d. 869), and that of the jurist Ibn Hanbal (780–855).

To the stories of the prophet, the Shi'i added those of the imams, whose teachings illustrated the significance of the prophetic message. The most important collection was that of Muhammad ibn Ya 'qub al-Kulayni (d. 939), which was known as the *Usul al-afi* (Foundations of the Compendium).

Nevertheless, the number of apocryphal *hadith* grew. False *hadith* had already appeared during the life of the Prophet. Because of the gravity of this problem, Islamic scholars created a method of exegesis known as '*ilm al-hadith* or science of the *hadith*, which was divided into two branches. The '*ilm al-djarh* specialized in the examination of the *hadith* and the '*ilm al-diraya* controlled the authenticity of their transmission. This exegesis resulted in a classification of *hadith* according to the criteria of the number of *isnad* in each *hadith* and to its intrinsic and extrinsic validity, referring to a lexicon specially formed during the course of the research.

When the authority is the Prophet himself, the *hadith* is known as *marfu'*, (raised); if it is that of a Companion, it is called *mawquf*. When it includes an unusual and strange expression, it is called *garib*. A very special sort of *hadith*, called *hadith qudsi* (holy tradition) was distinguished from the rest and was not submitted to the previous classifications. The text of the *hadith qudsi* is not attributed to the

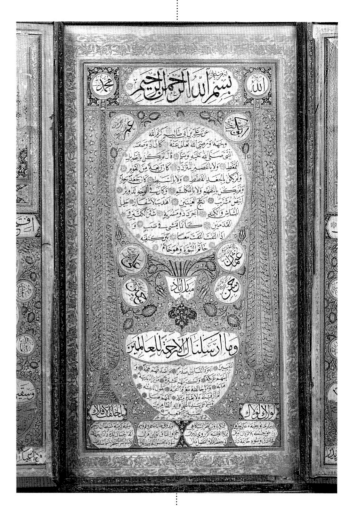

Prophet; it is the direct word of God entrusted to the inspiration of Muhammad and transmitted by him without commentary.

Detail of a Turkish triptych in wood with a description of the Prophet. Museo d'Arte Orientale, Rome.

The transmission of *hadith*.

Over a period of years, Abu Hurayra, loyal servant of the Prophet and who did not convert to Islam until 628, gathered together a collection of *hadith* larger than any other. He died in Medina in 678, having held important positions in the Islamic state. Another significant contribution came from 'Abdallah, the son of the second caliph, 'Umar. 'Abdallah died in Mecca in 692. *Hadiths* are also attributed to Anas ibn Malik, a figure of great interest, who entered the service of the Prophet at a very young age. His long life ended in 711, at Bassora. 'A'isha, Muhammad's favorite wife, who played an important role for Islam after the Prophet's disappearance, also transmitted a large number of *hadith*.

Two scholars. Syrian miniature (1229). Topkapi Saray Museum, Istanbul. The sunnah *contains exemplary episodes of the life of the Prophet. Therefore, from the study of the* sunnah, *the* shari'ah, *the Islamic Law, is derived.*

Below: *The slaughter of an animal. Detail from an ivory plaque. (Egypt, 11th –12th centuries). Museo del Bargello, Florence. Islam's laws governing the slaughter of animals are of Semitic origin.*

Through the enforcement and clarification of Qur'anic precepts, the science of Islamic jurisprudence, *fiqh*, developed. The role of the *fiqh* was to establish the knowledge of the laws of God that concern the actions of all responsible Muslims, classifying them from required to forbidden. The word *shari'ah* comes from a root which means marked path, meaning the clear and defined way which leads to God.

The *shari'ah* is the set of religious commandments which regulate the behavior of the Muslim in all of his private and social activities. The four foundations of the Islamic law are the Qur'an, the *sunnah* of the Prophet, and the substantial principles: the *qiyas*, (analogical deduction) and the *ijma'* (consensus or formal principal).

The *shari'ah* is divided into two parts: *'ibadat* (devotional acts), pertaining to an individual's spiritual relationship with Allah, and *mu'amalat* (human relationships). While the Prophet was alive, his authority was invoked to resolve any uncertainty. Under the four caliphs who succeeded him, the *sunnah* was applied. However, the administrative and legal practices that were in force in the pre-Islamic Byzantine and Sassanian empires had to be considered when planning the administration of a new and rapidly expanding state. Because the role of the caliphs was not to enforce the divine law, but to run the empire, the

Dietary regulations.
By Islamic law Muslims are forbidden to eat pork, blood, and the flesh of animals that are not slaughtered according to the Islamic rite. Islam did not markedly change the dietary habit from that of the pre-Islamic Arabs but did introduce ritual slaughter, which is of Semitic origin. The ritual involves pronouncing the Bismallah formula, "In the name of Allah", then cleanly slicing the throat of the animal and letting as much blood drain as possible. Meat from animals killed in this way are *halal*, (permitted). Over time, legal treatises enumerated a series of permitted and forbidden foods, with some variation, according to schools. The flesh of fish and locusts is authorized, even if the animal is already dead. Spilled blood

office of *qadi* (judge) was established. For the entirety of the Umayyad reign, these judges were in charge of enforcing obedience to the *shari'ah*.

The risk of moving progressively further from the Islamic principles necessitated the establishment of a legal body to rectify the situation. During the reign of the 'Abbasids, a process was initiated which would purify traditional Islamic law and codify laws which conformed to the teachings of the Qur'an and the prophetic *hadith*. The role of the *sunnah*, which was fundamental to legal reasoning, was extended by *a ra'y*, personal opinion of rational character. This was in turn reinforced by the *qiyas*, analogical deductions, which were made when a judge related a present situation to a previous one on which a ruling had already been taken. To avoid the possibility of dissension, one could turn to the *ijma'*, the unanimous consensus of Islamic law. The link between the *sunnah* and *ijma'* was made by *ijtihad*

(systematic original reasoning). The only people who were considered competent in this matter were the *'ulama'*, (scholars or religious scientists).

After the ninth century, the *ijma'* was confined to the recension of existing legal opinions. Absolute *ijtihad* were not allowed, except to great persons such as Ibn Taymiyyah (d. 1328), and only the right of relative *ijtihad* was authorized.

The multiplication of legal opinions led to the institution of *madhahib*, (legal schools.) The foundation of the first schools of the law is attributed to two great jurists: Abu Hanifah (700–767) from Kufa, Iraq, and Malik ibn Anas (712–795) from Medina. They carried out long and meticulous studies of the Qur'an and the *hadith*, referring constantly to the actions of the first generation of Companions.

Student at the University of Abu Dhabi, United Arab Emirates. The knowledge of the divine laws which guide the believer's behavior is called djiqh.

is forbidden, but the liver and the spleen are allowed. It is forbidden to eat all that has not been sacrificed to God. Dates are a favorite food of Muslims, and they are recommended for breaking a fast, following the Prophet's example. Alcohol is forbidden by

Islamic law according to the verse, "O believers, this wine and gambling, these idols, and these arrows you use for divination, are all acts of Satan; so keep away from them. You may haply prosper." (Qur'an 5: 90). Therefore, all fermented drinks, and drugs in

general, are forbidden. The *surah* extends the prohibition to all types of gambling and commands men to abstain from wearing silk clothing and gold ornamentation.

The study of texts in a Sunni theological school in Torbat-e Jam, Iran. According to the Sunni, Islamic law was decisively fixed in the 10th century, while for the Shi'i, the sayings of the imams hold legal validity.

Below: *The judge. Miniature by al-Wasity (1237). Bibliothèque nationale, Paris.*

Iraqi judges who enforced the *sunnah* of the Prophet were the first to link doctrine deriving from regional custom and consensus with the authority of Muhammad. Starting with these judges, the *hadith* began to hold greater importance and appeared more frequently in legal texts.

The authentic *a hadith* were collected and added to the *sunnah*. This became one of the bases of the *fiqh* after its level of authority was re-evaluated and estimated as inferior to that of the Qur'an.

Muhammad ibn Idris ash-Shafi (768–820), the great jurist and student of Malik ibn Anas, made a decisive step in the elaboration of the theory of Islamic law by founding the third Sunni legal school. He confirmed the value of the *ijma'* and of *qiyas* but challenged the validity of personal opinion. Ash-Shafi'i also rehabilitated the Tradition by restoring the *hadith* to a fundamental role in the establishment of the *shari'ah*. He definitively changed Islamic juris-

prudence by broadening the legal scope of reference that his predecessors had limited to the *'ulama'*, the competent authorities.

During the 'Abbasid period, differences of opinion on certain principals of the *shari'ah* degenerated into open conflict. The Caliph al-Ma'mun (813–833) forced the most eminent judges to accept the doctrine of the created Qur'an. Near the middle of the ninth century, an evolving political situation encouraged the creation of a fourth legal school. The traditionalist Ahmad ibn Hanbal (780–855) took a stand in favor of acceptance by faith of the "uncreated word of God." The teaching of Ibn Hanbal, which was greatly successful until the fourteenth century, was based uniquely on the Qur'an and the rejected *hadith*. The Wahhabis of the eighteenth century were inspired by this doctrine, which rejected a rational interpretation of the Revelation. Besides the authority of the Qur'an, this school only recognized

The Imams, interpreters of the law. According to the Shi'i, imams have attained a heightened level of knowledge and practice of the law. Their personal opinions concerning legal questions, or *ijtihad*, have the weight of law. The law is interpreted in the name of, and in the physical absence of, the twelfth Imam who is in *ghaybah* (hiding).

that of the *sunnah* (the source of the *shari'ah*) and of the *umma* (community), for which all decisions were made by the caliph. In spite of the existence of differing opinions regarding the foundations of the law, the importance given to the Tradition is a common trait held by all of the schools.

There are, therefore, four fundamental legal schools recognized by the Sunni. The Hanafi school, adopted by the 'Abbasids, became the official school of the Ottoman empire — becoming widespread in Turkey, the eastern part of the Arab world, India. and Pakistan. This is the most liberal school, claiming the adherence of approximately half of the Muslims.

The Maliki school is dominant in North Africa. The Shafi'i school, has always been present in Egypt and claims a small following in Syria, Bahrain, and Indonesia. The Hanbali school, which has a smaller number of disciples, has long been represented in Egypt and in Syria. It was from this school that the Wahhabi movement originated.

The creation of legal schools in the Shi'i world dates back to Ja'far al-Sadiq (699–765), the sixth Imam, who was a descendant of 'Ali. Differing from the Sunni, the Shi'i see the imams as the interpreters of the law, and their acts and sayings are of equal value to that of the *hadith*. However for the Sunni, the door of the *ijtihad* was closed, since the definitive organization of the four legal schools in the tenth century allowed little freedom to use the *ijma'*. Since the end of the *ijtihad* until the modern period, Sunni law has been regulated by the treatises of the *fiqh*. For all new and complicated cases, one may turn to the *fatwa* (religious opinion), expressed by the *faji* or *mufti* (a specialist in religious law). This role was not an innovation; Muslim governors had been appointing official *muftis* in the provinces and large cities for centuries. The *mufti* does not create laws; instead, he explains the regulations contained in the treatises of the *fiqh* and applies them to the case in question. For the *fiqh*, an act is legally classified

according to five values: *fard* (required), *mandub* (commendable), *mubah* (tolerated), *makruh* (reprehensible), and *haram* (strictly forbidden and punishable by the law).

Study in the prayer room of the Islamic Center of Rome.

Sunni and Shi'i.
The Sunni and Shi'i schools have several different opinion regarding specific teachings of the *shari'ah*, for example, questions of succession and the social position of women. Concerning political organization, for

the Shi'i, a perfect government cannot exist in the absence of the Mahdi (the twelfth, or "hidden", Imam), for the Sunni the caliphate is the legitimate form of government, since the caliph is the lieutenant of the Prophet and is responsible for enforcing

the divine law. When the Mongols took Baghdad, they destroyed the caliphate, the symbol of Islamic political unity. The *shari'ah* was thenceforth the sole remaining unifying factor for Islam.

Kula prayer rug (Anatolia, 17th century). The image of the mihrab on the rug is pointed towards Mecca. Prayer, one of the five Pillars of Islam, can be performed anywhere. Because of this, the prayer rug has a central role in the life of the Muslim.

Below: *Ablution of the feet which precedes entry into the mosque. Mosque of Muhammad 'Ali, Cairo.*

Islamic religious practice demands of the Muslim five essential requirements, or five *arkan* (pillars or foundations of faith). These are the profession of faith (*shahadah*), canonical prayer (*salat*), charity (*zakat*), the fast of Ramadan (*sawm*), and the pilgrimage to Mecca (*hajj*).

Shahadah
the profession of Faith.

In the order of priorities established by the *hadith* of the Prophet, the Muslim's first duty is the profession of faith. The *shahadah* requires more than the devotion of the believer; it is a formal act that consists of speaking the phrase, "I bear witness that there is no God but Allah and Muhammad is the Prophet of Allah." After a brief training, one may become a part of the Islamic community by reciting this declaration before witnesses, preceded by the *niyat* (the statement of intention).

The *niyat*
Required by the law, the *niyat* (statement of intention) has a fundamental role as the prelude to every religious act. None of these acts are considered valid, if the *niyat* has not first been recited.

Salat
the Prayer.

The most important duty of the Muslim is the *salat*, the daily ritual prayers. In Arabic the term does not mean a personal and spontaneous prayer from the heart, but rather a ritual, canonical worship.

There are five prayers, preceded by an *adhan* (the call), and by *wudu'* (ritual ablutions), which are necessary for the purification of the body and soul before presenting oneself before God. The clothes worn by the Muslim and the ground upon which he prays must also be clean.

Prayers are held at dawn, noon, mid-afternoon (at the midpoint between the sun's zenith and setting), at sunset, and after twilight. The Qur'an repeatedly mentions the requirement of canonical prayers, without specifying the details of the rite. "Be firm in devotion...and bow with those who bow (before God)." (Qur'an 2: 43).

In fact, the sequence of the *salat*, follows a ritual taught by the Prophet in his *hadith*: "Carry out prayer as you have seen me carry it out."

All Muslims who have reached puberty and are in full possession of their mental faculties are required to perform *salat*. After turning towards the *qibla*, (the direction of Mecca), the faithful must pronounce the *niyat*. This is followed by the *takbir*, the enunciation of the Allahu Akbar, (God is Great), in the position called *qiyam*, in which one stands with arms raised and hands held open at shoulder level. By pronouncing this phrase, the speaker enters a state of holiness and is forbidden to take any actions, other than praying, at the risk of nullifying the prayer.

Motionless in the *qiyam* position, the orator takes his left wrist in his right hand, and recites the Fatihah, first *surah* of the Qur'an. He closes with an extra-Qur'anic *amin*, followed by at least three short verses of the Qur'an of his own choice.

After the *takbir*, the orator bows forward with

palms posed on his knees in the *ruku'* position, and recites a brief formula of glorification three times. After straightening up, he then kneels in the *sujud* (prostration) position, placing his hands on the ground with his forehead on his hands, while repeating the formula of glorification three times.

This is followed by the *julus* (sitting) position, where the orator leans on his heels, squatting, with hands placed on the thighs. He performs another *sujud* with three "glorifications." This completes the first unit of prayer, or *rak'a*. The orator resumes the standing position and begins the second *rak'a*. At the end of all of the required *rak'a*, the orator stays on his knees, in the *julus* position, to recite the *tahiyyat* (the elegy of the Prophet), followed by the repetition of the *shahadah* (profession of faith). To conclude the prayer, he turns his head first to the right, then to the left while saying the *taslim* (the salutation of peace).

The dawn prayer consists of two *rak'a*, that of twilight consists of three and all others of four. The prayer can be made anywhere at the prescribed time, either alone or in a group, but congregational devotion is encouraged. The law demands that a congregational prayer be made in the mosque on Fridays at noon. It is preceded by the *khutba* (the religious and moral sermon) given by the *khatib* (preacher), who speaks from either a seated or standing position. Although traditional Islamic law considers Friday a holiday, work is not forbidden on this day. Other prayers, reserved for important holidays, are also required.

Zakat
the almsgiving tithe.

The third pillar of Islam, the *zakat* or (almsgiving tithe), is also an essential religious duty. As a kind of debt to God, the Muslim pays this tithe in exchange for the good things God has granted him. The payment of *zakat* purifies and

Prayer in a street of Baghdad. The man is in the sujud *(prostration) position.*

Below: *Page from a prayer book. The name of the Prophet is in red. Reading of the Qur'an, enunciation of the name of Allah and praise of the Prophet are a part of everyday life for all Muslims.*

legitimizes the Muslim's possessions. As with the other requirements, the Qur'an refers to the *zakat*, but the details are specified only in the *hadith* of the Prophet and in the law. The divine command is explicit: "Be firm in devotion, give *zakat* (the due share of your wealth for the welfare of others)" (Qur'an 2: 43).

The Qur'an also specifies the categories of people to whom alms must be given. "Charities are meant for the

Wudu' and *ghusl*, the purification.
Touching impure objects, such as the skin of an animal or a woman who is not a family member, carries with it a state of impurity. While impure, the Muslim is forbidden to pray, to circumambulate the

Ka'bah, and to come into physical contact with a copy of the Qur'an. The state of impurity is removed by the *wudu'*. Sexual relations during a woman's menstruation, as well as during the forty days which follow childbirth, are considered a major

impurity. This state is purged by the *ghusl* (major ablution), the equivalent of a bath.

Meditation in the Eyub Mosque, Istanbul.

Below: *The verse of the Qur'an concerning the* zakat.

those who are burdened with debt, and in the cause of God, and the wayfarers: So does God ordain. God is all-knowing and all-wise." (Qur'an 9: 60.)

The minimum tax on possessions is called *nisab*. This legally-regulated minimum is levied against profits of harvests, fruits, livestock, gold and silver, merchandise, and jewelry. When gold, silver, and merchandise are amassed, 2.5 percent per year of the current market value is deducted. (For example, the *nisab* for gold which was not earned in a commercial activity equals the value of 96 grams of gold, and according to this value, 2.5 percent would be collected.)

The tax on agricultural products is fixed at one tenth of the value, except when crops carry irrigation expenses, in which case it is reduced to a twentieth. Islamic jurisprudence regulates the tax on livestock with precision, according to a detailed scale. The same meticulousness is shown regarding all forms of

wealth from real estate, property, mining, or natural resources. It is specified by law that the tax collectors must be of high moral character, since they seek to encourage altruism among citizens who are able to act in favor of Islam but whose zeal towards the faith may still be weak. The tax can be given to slaves who desire their freedom and to debtors who contracted their debt for a worthy purpose but were not able to repay it. The rest must be contributed to the public good and to the cause of God, and finally, to aid pilgrims.

**Sawm
the fast.**

Fasting during the holy month of Ramadan is the second fundamental duty required of all Muslims, except in specific cases. The law exempts minors, the elderly, the mentally or chronically ill, those who fall ill during the fast, travelers, pregnant women or nursing mothers, and those for whom the fast could pose a risk. The fast is

Sadaqa and zakat
The Qur'an uses two terms to define charity: *sadaqa* and *zakat*. However, the *sadaqa* (voluntary giving) is legally distinguished from the *zakat*, the tax established by the law which "purifies" personal possessions.

indigent and needy, and those who collect and distribute them, and those whom you wish to win over, and for redeeming slaves (and captives) and

The requirement of the fast. The Qur'an commands Muslims to fast during the month of Ramadan in the verse, "O believers, fasting is enjoined on you as it was on those before you, so that you might become righteous." (Qur'an 2: 183).

The breaking of the fast.
An involuntary breaking of the fast does not carry any sanction, on the condition that one returns immediately to the fast after becoming conscious of the violation. When the fast is voluntarily breached,

forbidden to Muslim women who are menstruating or who are recovering from childbirth.

When the causes which justified abstention or interdiction cease, those who were exempted are required to make up the lost days. The foundations of the legal requirement to fast are set out in the Qur'an (2: 183-185) and were later established by the *shari'ah*. In addition, the law recognizes and recommends a voluntary fast on certain days of the year.

The Qur'an abolished embolism, the insertion of one or more days into the calendar. During the pre-Islamic epoch, this method was used to re-establish the balance between solar and lunar calendars every two or three years. The Qur'an changed this: "Intercalating a month is adding to unbelief. The unbelievers are misguided by this, for they take the same month to be sacred one year and sacrilegious the next, thus making the number of months sanctified by God accord with theirs in order

to make what God has forbidden, lawful. Attractive seem to them their evil deeds; but God does not show the unbelievers the way." (Qur'an 9: 37). On the basis of this verse, Islam returned to a strictly lunar calendar. Because the lunar calendar has alternate months of twenty-nine and thirty days, the lunar year has 354 days and is eleven days behind the solar calendar.

The law demands more than a simple calculation to proclaim the beginning of the month of Ramadan. Ramadan is only considered to have begun, when a credible witness testifies that he has seen the crescent moon.

Ramadan is the ninth month of the Islamic calendar and is held sacred in Islam. "Ramadan is the month in which the Qur'an was revealed as guidance to man and clear proof of the guidance, and criterion (of falsehood and truth)." (Qur'an 2: 185). It is a month of purification, rich with grace, and on one of the last nights, called *Laylat*

al-qadar (the Night of Destiny) it is believed that the doors of heaven are slightly ajar.

The fast is in effect from the first rays of dawn until twilight. It is generally preceded by a light meal, called *suhur*, taken just before daybreak in order to equip the devout to face the day. As with the salat, the fast is not valid unless it is preceded by the *niyat*. Once this is said, the fast begins (about fifteen minutes before the dawn

Prayer at the end of the fast, in front of the Aqsa Mosque in Jerusalem. The fast lasts from sunrise to sunset during the entire month of Ramadan, the ninth month of the Islamic calendar.

amends must be made, either by offering a meal to a certain number of indigent Muslims, by giving them the equivalent of the meal in money, or by fasting for sixty days.

The spiritual significance of the fast. The spiritual meaning is more important than the material, because, by keeping the fast, the Muslim is obeying a divine command. The fast teaches him to control his physical desires and overcome his lower nature.

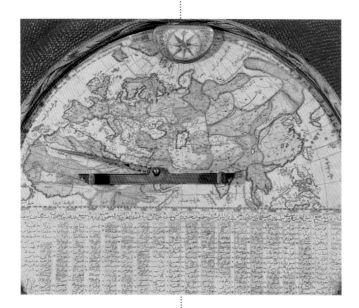

Detail of the cover of a compass used to calculate the exact direction of Mecca, from wherever the user was located (18th century). Museum of Turco-Islamic Art, Istanbul.

prayer). Obviously, the fast requires abstinence from all food and drink, but sexual relations and evil thoughts or actions are also prohibited from sunrise to sunset. Quarreling, lying, and slander are all strictly forbidden.

When the fast ends at sunset, abstinence is broken by eating dates and drinking water, as suggested in the *sunnah* of the Prophet. By tradition, a short prayer, *ifta*, precedes the breaking of the day's fast.

Traditionally, after the ritual prayer of the evening, a long evening prayer called the *tarawih* is said. According to the *sunnah* of the Prophet, this includes a minimum of eight *rak'a* and a maximum of twenty.

Ramadan is also a month of charity, during which the believer has the duty of sharing his goods with the needy. The fast ends when the new moon of the month of Shawwal appears. The abstinence is concluded, and the *'id al-fitr* (the feast of the breaking of the fast) is celebrated.

Hajj
the pilgrimage.

The pilgrimage to Mecca is the fifth pillar of Islam. Its performance is imperative and very strictly regulated. Each Muslim has the obligation to journey to Mecca at least once in his lifetime, if the necessary means are available. The rituals of the pilgrimage are very complicated. The Qur'an alludes to it in several *surah*, and precise

details are given by the *sunnah* and the Tradition — particularly the one which tells of the last pilgrimage of the Prophet in 632, not long before his death.

The pilgrimage is made between the eighth and thirteenth days of the month of Dhu al-Hijjah. As it is a medium for purification, the *hajj* is an important event in the believer's life. During the journey toward and around the House of God, the Muslim asks for the remission of sins and expresses repentance. The completion of the rites contribute to his purification: after carrying out the pilgrimage, the pilgrim is given the honorific title of *hajji* (or *hajjah* for women), and this commits them to living pious lives.

The rite of pilgrimage also effectively promotes social integration. For centuries, men and women of all races and all social classes from around the world have gathered in the place that symbolizes the

The months of the year. Each month in the Muslim calendar starts with the new moon. They are, in order: Muharram, Safar, Rabi' al-Awal, Rabi' at-Thani, Jamad al-Awal, Jamad at-Thani, Rajab, Sha'ban, Ramadan, Shawal, Dou al-Qidah, Dhu al-

Hijjah. They closely correspond to the solar months of January to December.

unity of the Islamic community.

The holy ground of Mecca, the *haram*, encompasses some of the surrounding countryside. Its limits were set by the Prophet himself. The five points of entry distributed around the borders of this holy space are known as *mauaqit*, (singular *miqat*). As soon as they arrive at the holy ground, at the *miqat* corresponding to their country of origin, the pilgrims must enter into a state of *ihram*, or ritual purity. They start with the *ghusl*, the major ablutions. The pilgrims trim their hair and fingernails, put on perfume, and clothe themselves in pilgrim's garb.

When performing the *'umrah* (or lesser pilgrimage), each pilgrim begins by reciting the *niyat*, without which it would be invalid. He must then announce his intention to obey the divine order to go to Mecca by loudly chanting the *talbiya* with the other pilgrims. This is performed during the trip

from the *miqat* to the sacred mosque, where the pilgrims enter through the Door of Peace. After entering the holy enclosure of the Ka'bah, at the height of the Black Stone, the pilgrims begin the *tawaf* (circumambulation), moving seven times counter-clockwise around the Ka'bah.

The central area of the pilgrimage is the Great Mosque of Mecca, which includes the Ka'bah and the Zamzam wells. The Ka'bah is a cubical building, situated almost in the middle of the mosque's immense courtyard. The Black Stone is embedded in its eastern corner, five feet above the ground. This block of black rock was already considered holy by Abraham and by the pre-Islamic Arabs. It is venerated because it was touched by the hands of the Prophet, but it is not an object of worship, nor does it hold the status of an idol.

Facing the Ka'bah is a two-story building containing the blessed spring of Zamzam. A little further is the *maqam of*

Abraham, (the station of Abraham), a small building near the Ka'bah where Abraham lived briefly. To the northwest of the mosque is the *mas'a* (the place of the procession), where the ceremonies of the *sa'yi* (the procession) between the hills of Safa and Marwa take place. This ritual commemorates Hagar's search for water and

Pilgrims at the Ka'bah in Mecca, Saudi Arabia. The Black Stone is ensconced in the eastern corner of the building.

Below: *Map of Mecca from the cover of a compass (17th century). Museum of Turco-Islamic Art, Istanbul.*

The call to pilgrimage. The Qur'an speaks of it in this way: "Announce the Pilgrimage to the people. They will come to you on foot and riding along distant roads on lean and slender beasts, / In order to reach the place of advantage for them, and to

pronounce the name of God on appointed days over cattle He has given them for food; then eat of the meat and feed the needs and the poor. / Let them attend to their persons and complete the rites of pilgrimage, fulfill their vows and circuit

round the ancient House." (Qur'an 22: 27-29).

The army of Muhammad marches against the infidels. Persian miniature. Bibliothèque nationale, Paris.

Below: *Around the Ka'bah, pilgrims are dressed in the required clothes of the pilgrimage.*

was suggested and carried out by the Prophet himself.

After completing the seventh turn around the Ka'bah, the believer leaves the area and proceeds to the station of Abraham. Once there, he says a prayer of four *rak'a*, then follows the path towards the hill of Safa. After saying three glorification formulas, the pilgrim walks the path between the two hills seven times. When finished, the men leave Marwa to cut their hair, or if they wish to respect the *sunnah* in the strictest sense, to shave their head. The *'umrah* is concluded with this act, and the *ihram* (state of ritual purity) ends.

The difference between the *'umrah*, (lesser pilgrimage) and the *hajj* (the great pilgrimage), is that the rites of the *hajj* can be carried out only during a fixed period of time. After arriving at the *miqat*, the believer says the *niyat* and enters the state of *ihram*. He then moves towards the Great Mosque of Mecca for the noon *salat*, where he attends a sermon dedicated

to the duties of the pilgrim. The second day, the ninth day of the holy month of Dhu al-Hijjah, the pilgrim leaves for the plain in front of Mount Arafat, approximately four hours east of Mecca by camel, stopping for noon prayer at Mina, a place between the two. According to the *sunnah*, this journey, called "the Day of Arafat," is the culminating moment of the pilgrimage. The pilgrims gather together on the plain near the mountain, and, from the beginning of the afternoon until sunset, enter into prayer and worship, repeating loudly, "Here am I God! Here am I!" At sunset, the pilgrims leave the plain of Arafat and head towards Muzdalifah, where they spend the night of the ninth day.

Just before dawn, another celebration takes place, similar to that at Arafat, which ends with a race, *ifada*, to reach Mina before sunrise. There, the pilgrims carry out the "Stoning of Satan," where seven stones are hurled against a slab

while the appropriate phrase is spoken.

The tenth day of Dhu al-Hijjah is the day sacrifices are made in memory of Abraham. The meat of the sacrificed animals is, for the most part, distributed to poor people. After this, the pilgrims return to Mina, where the men cut their hair or shave their heads, and the women trim theirs by a few inches.

At this point, the interdictions imposed under the state of purity are lifted, with the exception of sexual relations. The pilgrims go to Mecca for the circumambulations and the *sa'yi* between the two hills. During the eleventh, twelfth and thirteenth days, the pilgrims travel to Mina where, each afternoon, they ritually stone the three rock slabs representing Satan, starting with the smallest. The departure from Mina must be made before sunset. Before leaving the holy places, the pilgrims return to the Ka'bah for the Circumambulation of Farewell. There are many similarities between the *hajj* and the *'umrah*. Regarding

The 'umrah and the hajj. There are two sorts of pilgrimages: the lesser, the *'umrah*, and the great, the *hajj*. The *'umrah* can take place at any time, but if it is carried out during Ramadan it acquires the same religious value as the great pilgrimage.

The pilgrim's dress. Men wear two lengths of white fabric, clean and unsewn. The cloth which wraps around the hips, under the torso, is called *izar*, the other, the *rida*, covers the upper half of the body, leaving the right shoulder bare. Women must

wear a flowing garment, of white fabric, if possible, which leaves their face and hands bare.

the *hajj*, the Prophet said, "Only paradise can reward a pilgrimage accepted by Allah."

The jihad a sixth pillar?

Like the five pillars of Islam prescribed by the *shari'ah*, the *jihad* is fundamental, but it depends on circumstances and is not a personal duty. It is always considered *fard kifayah* (a collective duty), carrying the deeper meaning of a "struggle accomplished on the Path and for the cause of God." The usual definition of *jihad* as "great holy war" overlooks the internal dimension: a constant struggle against evil and bad habits must be waged by each Muslim.

The *jihad's* initial meaning of an internal combat was explained well by the Prophet. *Al-jihad al-akbar* is "the ascetic struggle on the path of God," and *al-jihad al-asghar* is "the minor struggle, a struggle of combat on the Path of God." Islam teaches that this effort to affirm the supremacy of the Word of

God, which is a noble and lofty goal, must not be carried out by ignoble and abject methods. To carry the reward of salvation, the *jihad* must be conducted according to the regulations of the law. In all cases, the law precludes the murder of women, children, the elderly, monks, and the defenseless in general. In addition, it forbids the destruction of the property and homes of the enemy.

The law also defines the rules for dividing the booty of war and enumerates a number of arrangements which prevent recourse to terrorism, oppression, violence and abuse. In this sense, acts of terrorism are never in any manner in keeping with the laws concerning *jihad*.

In an Iranian village. Procession with nakhale, *a sort of canopy that displays the portraits of martyrs in God's cause. The procession takes place at the end of the month of Muharram, in memory of the martyrdom of the third Imam, Husayn, in 680.*

***Kuffar* and *ahl al-kitab*.**
The Qur'an makes a clear distinction between the true *kuffar* (infidels) and the *ahl al-kitab* (people of the Book), the adherents of the pre-Islamic revelation-based religions tolerated by Islam. These included

Judaism, Christianity and Sabeism as well as, in certain cases, Zoroastrianism. When the *ahl al-kitab* came under Islamic domination, their faith, religions, and sanctuaries were respected on the condition that they pay the tribute, the *jizya*,

which corresponded closely in value to the *zakat* paid by the Muslims.

Mother and daughter, and, to the right, little girls in a school in an Iraqi village.

Below: *A young boy wears the traditional ceremonial costume for circumcision. Istanbul.*

Because of its tribal organization and an inhospitable environment, pre-Islamic Arab society was built on a patriarchal system in which women were relegated to a secondary role. The birth of a girl was not welcomed, especially if she were not the first in the family. Girls were considered as extra mouths to feed, and, because they were not useful in times of combat, they were seen as dishonoring their family.

This attitude was not adopted by Islam, but the attachment to patriarchal customs and masculine privilege has propagated attitudes that are difficult to overcome. Indeed, of all the children fathered by the Prophet, only the girls survived, and he was very fond of them. He frequently confided in Fatimah and spoke to her in these terms, "You are the one who resembles me most." He also said, "A person who, having had two daughters and having treated them well so that they live close to him, will enter Paradise thanks to them."

At the moment of birth, tradition has it that the *azan* (the call to prayer) and several verses of the Qur'an are softly recited in the child's right ear, followed by the *iqamah* (the second call), in the left ear.

A name is then chosen. The Prophet said, "The name which you give, may it begin with 'Abd (servant)." Even a stillborn child must be given a name.

It is required that two sheep be sacrificed for the birth of a boy and only one for the birth of a girl. However, the Maliki school considers that the sacrifice of one animal is sufficient, whatever the sex of the newborn. Alms must also be distributed to the poor. In general, the sacrifice takes place the seventh day after birth, the day that the child receives its name.

This is also the day that circumcision is performed

Circumcision.
The Qur'an does not mention circumcision, but it is a very ancient practice used by several Semitic peoples, including Egyptians, Phoenicians, Abyssinians, Arabs, and Hebrews. In the rural milieu, circumcision is usually practiced at home by an expert or a nurse, but in towns it is often performed at a medical clinic.

(although it can be performed later, at the age of one or two years). The parents give the child the rudiments of religious education. After this, all members of society participate in the child's instruction, because the religious life is believed to be one and the same as social life.

Death

At the onset of death, several verses of the Qur'an are recited to the dying person, who pronounces the *shahadah* (the profession of faith.)

After death, the law requires that the deceased be given a funerary ablution, and that the corpse be wrapped in an unsewn *kafan* (shroud.) A series of *salat al-janaza* are said, followed by "the prayer for the dead," even in the absence of an imam. Women are allowed to participate in the prayer, but public expression of grief (weeping, crying out, and so forth) is forbidden.

The deceased is buried, lying on his right side, in the direction of Mecca. After the burial, the

mourners recite the *talqin*, in which they "suggest" the statement of faith to the dead person, so that he can correctly respond to Nakir and Munkir, the two angels he will meet on the other side of the grave.

A funeral banquet is often given between the seventh and the fortieth day after death, avoiding the three days of the *'aza'* (the funeral solace), during which those close to the deceased receive

condolences and attend a reading of the Qur'an at the mosque, under a canopy in the street, or at the house of the deceased.

The Qur'an and the Tradition describe the afterlife. Hell is an abyss of fire, while Paradise is a garden which includes sexual pleasures. The Qur'an speaks of *houris* (virgins of great beauty).

Muslim cemetery at Rabat, Morocco.

Left: *Muslim funeral in Karbala, Iraq. At the center, in dark clothing, is the Shi'i imam. The Qur'an describes in great detail what awaits man in the afterlife.*

Below: *Prayer in a cemetery in Istanbul.*

The prayer for the dead. The prayer must be recited while standing, starting with the *niyat*, and is followed by four *takbir*, the *Allahu Akbar*, with the hands lifted only on the first recitation. Certain schools allow the reading of the *surah* Fatihah, "the Prologue", after the first *takbir*. The second *takbir* is followed by the Elegy of the Prophet, and the third by a *du'a'*, (prayer from the heart), ending with an invocation of mercy and the forgiveness of God for the deceased. After the fourth *takbir*, another *du'a'* is said. Finally the orator nods to the right and the left, as is done at the end of the canonical prayer.

A Tunisian bride and groom pose for their wedding photo. The bride wears a traditional costume.

Below: Iraqi family at Karbala. The man wears the typical white robe, the thaub, *and a keffieh. The woman wears a black cloak, the* 'abayah.

Marriage is encouraged by Islam, in both the Qur'an and in the *sunnah* of the Prophet, especially because Muhammad was married. The Qur'an considers marriage a benefit, which should be sought after. The statement, "Marry off those who are single among you..." (Qur'an 24: 32), is taken as a commandment. God also said, "... do not stop them (divorced women) from marrying other men..." (Qur'an 2: 232).

The wife is considered as her husband's other half, and their marriage must involve love: "Another of His signs is that he created mates of your own kind of yourselves so that you may get peace of mind from them, and has put love and compassion between you." (Qur'an 30: 21).

In the Tradition given by the Prophet, the subject of marriage was spoken of extensively. Muhammad said, "Marriage is a part of my *sunnah*. He who does not follow the *sunnah* does not follow me." And, to encourage Muslims to marry, he also said, "Marry between you, and join together, and I will, at Judgment Day, place you

above all of the other nations, even the stillborn."

One of the *hadith* condemns all who find reasons to justify abstention from marriage: "Those who renounce marriage for fear of the responsibilities of the family are not a part of us." In Islam, marriage is seen as an aid to avoid the sin of illicit sexual relationships. On this subject, the Prophet said, "May they who are in a position to have carnal relationships marry; in this way one will avoid lustful looks and sexual disorders."

The pre-Islamic Arabs practiced unrestricted polygamy. Although the Qur'an allows polygamy, it is regulated by limiting the number of permitted wives to four. The Islamic conception of polygamy is spelled out in the Qur'an and precisely defined by the law. "...then marry women who are lawful for you, two, three or four; but if you fear you cannot treat so many with equity, marry only one, or a maid or captive. This is better than being iniquitous." (Qur'an 4, v. 3). The polygamous husband must not favor one wife to the detriment of the others. If he can not respect

this requirement, he is forbidden to take multiple wives. The law forbids marriage to those who are not capable of carrying out its duties. Far from being a right, polygamy is a privilege which carries with it certain conditions. Before giving or refusing his consent, the *qadi*, or any other competent authority, examines the social situation and possessions of anyone who wishes to take more than one wife. During the establishment of a marriage contract, the bride has the option of imposing a monogamy clause. The husband can still take another wife, but only in very particular conditions: if the wife is gravely ill or sterile, or if she is not able to respect the obligations of marriage.

From the Islamic religious point of view, marriage is not a sacrament but rather a simple rite. It is a legal contract between the husband and the *wali* (the matrimonial guardian), the legal representative of the wife (in absence of a *wali*, she becomes the responsibiltiy of authorities).

Islamic law stipulates the necessity of the woman's

Restriction of polygamy.

The historical context of the birth of Islam provides the reasons for polygamy: the principal being to encourage the birth-rate. In warlike cultures, the proportion of women to men was unbalanced, yet

men were nevertheless indispensable providers for women and children in a society, in which the woman did not work outside of the home. Today, polygamy is officially forbidden only in Tunisia. Morocco is attempting to abolish it, while in Egypt

and Syria it is discouraged by legal means. In general polygamy is disappearing in the Islamic world, except in tribal societies, in the peasant class, and in wealthy circles.

consent in order to marry (even though, in certain cases, it authorizes the father to force his daughter to marry against her will). On the other hand, a father cannot force his daughter to remain unmarried.

It is common practice that the marriage contract is established before the *qadi* or one of his delegates, and in the presence of two trustworthy witnesses. Thus, the marriage is not necessarily celebrated in a mosque; it can also be performed at home. The consent is voiced by the groom and the guardian, and it must include the words, *nikah* (wedding) and *tazwij* (marriage). The law requires a *mahr* (a dowry), which the groom solemnly promises to pay his bride. The Prophet discouraged claims to extravagant dowries: "The best wives are those of the most gracious mien and smallest dowry." Islam requires the husband to behave fairly (to show caring, to treat his wives as equals, and to provide for their upkeep, and to respect customs like the wedding banquet).

Marriage is forbidden in the case of a close blood relationship, as well as between two persons suckled by the same wet nurse, because a wet nurse is considered the equivalent of a mother.

The law tolerates marriage of Muslims with women who are *ahl al-kitab* (people of the Book), but Muslim women are not allowed to marry non-Muslims. This is because the man holds authority over the woman, and the children belong to the father.

Termination of a marriage is allowed; in fact, it is very easy to secure, but, according to the Qur'an, it is the most repugnant behavior. Divorce is allowed if it does not involve too much harm. The Prophet said, "The thing most hated in the eyes of God is divorce." Apart from the death of one of the couple, the dissolution of a marriage can only be effected in one of three ways: the *talaq,* (repudiation of the wife by the husband); the *khul* (redemption of the wife), in which the money given to her husband must not exceed the dowry; or by *faskh* (declaration of an annulment by the judge for specific circumstances). If

the wife does not possess the money necessary for her redemption, she can go to the *qadi* and submit her case. He can free her from this payment, if she is the one who has been wronged; but this type of judgment is difficult to receive. The woman can, for example, obtain a divorce if her husband must serve a long prison sentence or has been absent too long because of his job. Concerning redemption, the Qur'an says, "... there will be no blame on either if the woman redeems herself." (Qur'an 2: 229).

Bride and groom in Curepipe, Mauritius. According to a practice that is becoming more common, the bride and groom wear western clothing and hold sumptuous receptions which often take place in large hotels. These customs have nothing to do with Islamic teaching and practices.

Divorce. One of the features of Islamic divorce is that it is only considered final at the end of three successive breaches. A man cannot marry his wife again unless she has, in the meantime, married another man, called *muhallil,* who has himself divorced her. In every case, the law recommends that the husband behave amicably as soon as the breach is made and avoids mistreating or scorning his wife. In the Qur'an, God says, "but do not forget to be good to each other..." (Qur'an 2: 237) ("good", in this case, meaning "generous"). This "generosity" is obligatory in cases where the marriage is dissolved before it is consummated, and the sum of the dowry has not yet been paid.

The status of women

Student at the University of Istanbul, Turkey. Islam has never discouraged women from undertaking higher education, but it has prevented them from expressing legal opinions or holding positions that would give them authority over men. Nonetheless, in some Islamic countries, women have held high offices: they have been heads of company, lawyers and university professors and prime ministers.

Below: *Young Iraqi girl.*

The Qur'an directly addresses the status of women: "Women also have recognized rights as men have..."; and it adds, "...though men have an edge over them." (Qur'an 2: 228). Because of the weight of traditions and prejudices having nothing to do with religious law, the condition of women in Islamic countries is often less favorable than that which the Qur'an prescribes. Donning of the veil for example, is not explicitly required by the Qur'an and has never been adopted by the law. The law mentions it, but only as a custom of secular origin.

The condition of women remained practically unchanged for thirteen centuries, since it was legally organized in a firm manner by the Qur'an and the *sunnah*. Toward the end of the nineteenth century, several Muslim intellectuals (Egyptians, Turks, North Africans and Caucasians) started to speak of the status of women. Influenced perhaps by a journey to Europe, the Egyptian Qasim Amin (1863–1908) tackled questions of polygamy, divorce, and the veil in his book *The Liberation of Women* (1899). He wrote, "The Islamic law preceded all other legislation in proclaiming equality between men and women. It established liberty and independence for woman when no other nation gave her any rights. It gave her the same rights as men and allowed woman with the enjoyment of legal rights in no way inferior to that of man...."

In the years that followed, a feminist movement was born, led by two Egyptian women, Malak Hini Nasif and Hoda Sharawi. The latter protested in a dramatic fashion by tearing off her veil in the train station of Cairo in 1933.

Since then, a large number of Muslim women have occupied high social and political positions, but, on the whole, the status of women has not evolved. For example, a woman is still subject to the authority of her father, brothers, and husband.

Muslim tradition continues to view women as objects of temptation, and the menstrual cycle is still perceived as an impurity. Current advocates of women's liberation, such as the Egyptian Nawal Sa'dawi and the Moroccan Fatima Mernissi, rely on reinterpretations of the Qur'an and the *sunnah* to support their claims.

The Qur'an firmly defends women's right to life: "Yet when the news of the birth of a daughter reaches one of them, his face is darkened, and he is overwhelmed with silent grief, And hides from people for shame at the news, (at a loss) whether he should keep her with shame, or bury her in the

Right of inheritance. Regarding the rights of women to inheritance, the Qur'an says, "Men have a share in what the parents and relatives leave behind at death; and women have a share in what the parents and relatives leave behind. Be it large or small a legal share if fixed. [...] As for the children, God decrees that the share of the male is equivalent to that of two females..." (Qur'an 4: 7 and 11). Men receive twice as much as women because of their different social responsibilities. When a man marries, he assumes responsibility for the needs of his wife and children.

ground. How bad is the judgment that they make!" (Qur'an 16: 58-59).

The question of adultery in general is covered in Surah 24: 2-4. "The adulteress and adulterer should be flogged a hundred lashes each, and no pity for them should deter you from the law of God, if you believe in God and the Last Day; and the punishment should be witnessed by a body of believers. / The adulterer can marry no one but an adulteress or his partner (in the act), and the adulteress cannot marry any but an adulterer or her partner (in the act). This is forbidden the believers. / Those who defame chaste women and do not bring four witnesses should be punished with eighty lashes, and their testimony should not be accepted afterwards, for they are profligates..."

To be enforced, the stoning for *zina* (fornication), requires that four witnesses can testify to having seen the adultery with their own eyes and at the same time. These conditions have made punishment a deterrent more than a real danger.

Many consider the veil

to be a serious obstacle to women's rights in Islam. In fact, on this point, the Qur'an's guidance is rather hazy: "Oh Prophet, tell your wives and daughters, and the women of the faithful, to draw their wraps a little over them. They will thus be recognized and no harm will come to them. God is forgiving and kind." (Qur'an 33: 59).

From the Islamic point of view, the role and status of women in society accord with feminine nature. The natures of men and women are different (not antagonistic but complementary) and to each sex fall different tasks and duties. Even if a man's wife is rich, he bears the responsibility to support his family. This example was provided by the Prophet after his marriage to the rich and noble Khadijah. His favorite wife, 'A'ishah, said that when he wasn't working, the Prophet participated in familial duties.

In comparison to the conditions of pre-Islamic society, Islam has liberated women by giving them an important role to play. It is undeniable, however, that Islamic men benefit from

certain privileges, which originated in the historical context of the birth of Islam. The demands of social progress have made a re-evaluation of certain aspects of the condition of women inevitable, in conformity with the *shari'ah* and with the divine light of Islam.

Woman wearing the hijab *in a town of Iran.*

Below: *Veiled woman, Marrakech, Morocco.*

Mahram. A man can see unveiled only those female relatives whom he is forbidden to marry (or has already married). They are called *mahram*, and include his mother, sister, wife, mother-in-law, daughter-in-law (either son's wife or step-daughter), and all

other relatives of direct ascent or descent. The law grants the status of free man to children born from slaves and their masters.

Hijab. The veil is a barrier against sexual aggression. Woman's body is considered *ara* (bare), that is, vulnerable and without defense. In contrast to the heavy *neqab*, the semi-transparent *hijab* does not turn a woman into a shadow without a face.

Right: Street in Cairo lit up for the birthday of Muhammad.

Below: Prayer at the Islamic Center in Rome. There are specific prayers are given for each holiday, and the faithful must perform certain religious acts before enjoying the festivities.

There are two Islamic holidays that are more important than all others. The first is the *'id al-saghir*, which falls at the end of the month of Ramadan, starting on the first day of Shawal. It holds deep meaning for Muslims, since it ends their difficult trial during the fast. It is also called *'id al-fitr*, the celebration of the breaking of the fast, as the Muslims celebrate their personal success during this time. It is a holiday which places an emphasis on brotherhood, since on this occasion, whoever has the means, pays the *sadaqa*, the voluntary tax of the breaking of the fast.

The second most important feast day is the *'id al-adha* (Great Feast), which is held on the tenth day of Dhu al-Hijjah, at the same time as the sacrifices are made during the pilgrimage to Mecca. Consequently, it is also called the Feast of Sacrifices or Feast of the Sheep. On this occasion, Muslims across the world join in the joy of the pilgrims who have accomplished their duty of

the *hajj*. The festival commemorates Abraham's sacrifice of Ishmael (not of Isaac, as in the Bible). For the Great Feast, Muslims are encouraged to sacrifice a cow and distribute a part of it to the poor.

Tradition attributes the origin of these two feasts to the Prophet, who instituted them in place of two feasts that had been celebrated in Medina. In the words of the Prophet, "God has sent you two feasts better than those." They are occasions of joy and festivity as well as times of worship. During these feast days, a special prayer is recited, called *salat*

al-'id, or prayer of feast days.

Other, extra-canonical holidays are celebrated in the Muslim world. The first day of the Islamic year, the first of Muharram, is celebrated but holds less importance than New Year in the Christian world. The tenth day of the same month commemorates the death of Husayn, the son of 'Ali. The historian Ibn Khatir (1300–1372) tells in *al-Bidaya wa an-nihaya*, (Beginning and End), how it was decided in 963 at Baghdad to commemorate Husayn's martyrdom. During the first days of the

Holiday prayers.
The prayers said on the occasion of the two most important holidays of the year are very similar to the canonical Friday prayers. They are composed of two *rak'a*, led by an imam. First comes a *takbir*, which is followed by an opening

prayer and seven other *takbir*. The imam then reads the Fatihah, followed by several verses of the Qur'an and the first *rak'a*, as is the custom with regular prayers. He then says six *takbir* before starting the second *rak'a*, which are repeated by the congregation.

Religious holidays

month of Muharram, canopies are decorated, markets are closed, and people in robes of mourning recite prayers in honor of the Prince of Martyrs. Elegies and funeral songs are sung, lamenting the death of assassinated heroes, and ancient Arab ceremonial rites are given a religious dimension. Works in verse or in prose that glorify the sacrifice of martyrs are recited and enacted in passion plays, called 'Ashura' or Ta'ziyah.

The twelfth day of Rabi 'al-Awal, the third month of the year, is *al-mawlid al-nabi*, the birth of the Prophet. Prince Muzaffar al-Din al-Arbili (d. 1233) presided over the first large scale commemoration of this holiday, by gathering together scholars, scientists, poets, and preachers from across the empire. After this, the custom of celebrating this day spread throughout the Islamic world. The Prophet's praises are sung, and readings of his biography are sometimes accompanied by rhythmic swaying. In tents pitched especially for the holidays, poems and prose are recited

in honor of the Prophet's birth, alternating with litanies and praises. The guests exchange good wishes and have cakes and drinks.

The *mi'raj*, the night of the Prophet's Ascension, is celebated on the twenty-seventh day of Rajab. The event, mentioned in the Qur'an, and expanded on in the Tradition, is celebrated by all-night readings from the Sacred Book. During the last odd-numbered nights of

Ramadan, the revelation of the Qur'an is celebrated. One of these nights is the *laylat al-qadar*, (the Night of Determination). The Qur'an described it thus: "Better is the Night of Determination than a thousand months," (Qur'an 97: 3).

Mosque of Husayn, Karbala, Iraq. Shi'i believers flagellate themselves during the celebration of the anniversary of Husayn's death.

Below: *Husayn's horse in a popular contemporary woodcut engraving.*

The commemoration of the death of Husayn. Husayn's death is celebrated in diverse ways in different countries. Various texts are read. The most common is that of the Persian H. Va'ir Kashify (d. 1505) called *Hadiqat al-Shouhada,* The Garden of

Martyrs. Each year on the tenth day of the month of Muharram, the battle of Karbala is re-enacted. This pageant, while spectacular in Iran, involves less pomp and circumstance in Iraq and Lebanon, and is even less ostentatious in Egypt and Syria.

127

View of the Kodiamin Mosque in Baghdad, Iraq. The Shi'i movement is constituted upon the recognition of the authority of imams.

Below: *The hand of Fatimah in a popular Iraqi engraving. In Shi'a, the wife of 'Ali, Fatimah, is the object of great veneration.*

Shi'a claims to be a school of Islam and has developed its own legal and theological doctrine. Like the *sunnah*, it proposes an orthodox interpretation of the Islamic revelation, and because it is better suited to certain mentalities, it has helped make Islam a universal religion.

The two schools diverge principally on the question of the succession of the Prophet and his political and religious role. The question of succession had not been clearly resolved at the time of Muhammad's death. One group maintained that the position must rest in the family and supported 'Ali, cousin and son-in-law of the Prophet, but the majority were in favor of Abu Bakr. The fact that he was chosen, according to the Sunni, allowed him to be called *Ahl al-sunnah wa-l djama'a* (the Relative by Tradition and Consensus). Finally, 'Ali acceded to the caliphate in 657, following the successive reigns of three *al-Khulafâ' ar-Râchiodun* (Rightly-Guided Caliphs). He immediately went to war against Mu'awiya, governor of Syria and head of the Umayyad clan, who also claimed the caliphate. As soon as the tide of battle turned in his favor, 'Ali agreed to a request for *tahkim* (arbitration), which proved unfavorable to him. 'Ali has been often deified among the group of his faithful followers, called Shi'a, party or faction of 'Ali. A great number of his followers objected to his acceptance of the arbitration and abandoned him, because, according to them, the only true judge is God. These zealots formed the Khariji sect, or secessionists. They turned against 'Ali and the Umayyad dynasty as well. Their radical puritanism and their use of terrorism strengthened the conformity of the religious leaders of the Sunni, leading to the creation of the class of *'ulama'* (religious scholars.) Beginning in the ninth century loyalty to the *sunnah* and to the use of consensus acquired doctrinal status.

In opposition to the Sunni idea of *ijma'* (consensus), another group of the Shi'a advanced the doctrine of divine right. This doctrine, which did not challenge Muhammad's role as prophet, was nonconformist in that it refused to bow to the *ijma'*. Instead, it recognized the person of the imam, who was vested with divinely sanctioned authority and power.

Following the assassination of 'Ali at Kufa, this group insisted that the caliphate remain in 'Ali's family. Husayn, 'Ali's youngest son was overthrown at Karbala in 680 by the Umayyad troops of Yazid, Mu'awiya's successor. Husayn's violent death introduced the theme of suffering and

Mukhtar.
In the heart of Shi'a, Kufa, Iraq, Mukhtar encouraged Muhammad ibn Hanafiyyah, to rebel against the Umayyads. Muhammad was a son of 'Ali, but not of Fatimah, born of a marriage after her death. Mukhtar succeeded in seizing Kufa, but his rebellion failed in 687, when Muhammad pulled out of the alliance.

The School of the Twelve Prophets.
It is also called *Ja'fari*, after the sixth Imam, Ja'far al-Sadiq, founder of the Shi'i legal school, considered as the fifth Islamic school of law. The Shi'a duodeciman is close to the Sunni *shari'ah*, except in that

martyrdom as heroic qualities in Shi'ism. Within several years, Shi'ism, which was originally a political and social movement, founded a school of law with its own theology.

After a series of failed rebellions, the unity of the Shi'i movement formed around the recognition of the authority of imams descending from Husayn, son of 'Ali.

The conversion to Islam of new peoples and the subsequent contact with different religions and civilizations (including Christianity, Manicheism, Buddhism, and Greek philosophy) allowed the concept of the imamate to develop. For the Sunni, the caliph is only the guide of the community, whereas for the Shi'a, he is at the same time the *wali*, the heir and interpreter of esoteric and religious knowledge. One of the characteristics of Shi'ism is that it leaves the door open to the *ijtihad* (the creative thought of the individual) and the individual interpretation of dogma and of the Law. There are divisions among the Shi'i schools, about the number of imams that they

A Shi'i imam. Karbala, Iraq.

Below: *Prayer stone. In Shi'i worship, the believer sets a round stone, a* turba, *in front of him, and presses his forehead to it during prostration. It symbolizes the earth on which was spilled the blood of the martyr, Husayn.*

recognize after 'Ali and his son.

The school of twelve imams (the Imamiyyah School) has the greatest number of followers, and its position in religious tradition is the most prominent. There are two other schools (that of the seven imams, or Isma'iliyyah, and that of five imams, or Zaydiyya). The twelfth and last Imam, Muhammad al-Mahdi, the Rightly-Guided, having disappeared in mysterious circumstances, is known as the Hidden Imam. The Imamites do not only believe that the *ghaybah*

(the one in hiding, also called *al-muntazar*, the awaited one) is only spiritually present, but that he is actually living on earth in a secret location and will reappear at the end of time. He is also considered the *Sahib al-Zaman*, (the Lord of Time), capable of making his will known by different methods. After his disappearance, the community chose as their guide a *wakil* (lieutenant), or *bab* (door) who stayed in contact with the Hidden Imam. However, theologians of the Shi'a consider that the link with

which concerns the concept of the imamate. For example, included with the *zakat* is the *khums* (the fifth), a tax levied on booty, mines, and treasures. Another example is the *I'tikaf* (spiritual retreat), which should last for three days and three nights. The

jihad, (struggle in the path of God or holy war) is considered as one of the pillars of the faith, and can even be called for against Muslims who refuse to submit to the legitimate imamate. A type of marriage characteristic of the Shi'i is called the *muta*,

(temporary marriage). A pre-determined length of time is mentioned in the contract, after which period the marriage is automatically dissolved.

Karbala. The inner courtyard of the Mausoleum of Husayn. Son of 'Ali and Fatimah, the favorite daughter of the Prophet, Husayn was killed in 680 during the Battle of Karbala against the Umayyad army.

the Hidden Imam was broken at the death of the fourth and last *wakil* in 940. This also ended the *ghaybah sughra* (the lesser occultation) and started the *ghaybah kubra* (the greater occultation.) This period of occultation will end with the return of the Hidden Imam, who will re-establish the reign of justice and divine authority at the end of time. While waiting for this event, the doctors of the law have the power to make laws, on the basis of the Qur'an and of the Tradition concerning 'Ali and his descendants.

Shi'a teachings spread through Persia, where it became the most important school (after its proclamation as the official doctrine of the state in 1502 by the Savafids). Today it has ninety million followers, mostly in Iran, but also in Iraq, Pakistan, India, and in the Far East.

The quarrel over the succession of the sixth Imam, Ja'far al-Sadiq, who died at Medina in 765, introduced the first great division inside the Shi'a faith. Al-Sadiq's eldest son and legitimate successor, Isma'il, was considered

unworthy, and the majority nominated his youngest son, Musa, as imam. After his death, a small group of loyalists to Isma'il supported the claim of his brother, Muhammad, to the imamate as the seventh and last imam, destined to become the Hidden Imam. His followers were called Isma'iliyyah. Near the end of the ninth century, this branch of the Shi'a assumed a considerable importance throughout the Islamic world from North Africa to India. Its expansion was, in part, due to the revolt started in Kufa, Iraq, by Hamdan Karmat, which has been called the Karmate Insurrection. This anti-caliphal rebellion posed a major threat to the 'Abbasid power, which was already seriously weakened, and sparked warfare in the Arabian peninsula and among the Berber tribes of North Africa. In 909, the Aghlabid dynasty, loyal to the 'Abbasids, was chased from Kairouan, Tunisia, by the Isma'ili pretender, 'Ubaydallah, and his army of followers. He created the Fatimid caliphate by claiming direct descent from Fatimah, daughter of

Druzism and Nizarism. These two branches derive from Ismail'ism. The Druze sect deifies the Fatimid Caliph al-Hakim (996–1021). The Druze await his return as Mahdi at the end of time.

Today, the Druze have several hundred thousand

followers in Syria, Lebanon and Israel. The other branch sided with Nizar, the son of Caliph al-Mustansir, (d. 1094), in the fight over succession. Under the leadership of the *da'i*, (he who presents the truth), Fatimid Hasan ibn al-Sabbah (1090–1124),

who promoted the sect's spread in eastern countries (particularly in Persia), the Nizaris gave birth to a terrorist movement known as the *hachaychin* (Assassins). Their reign of fear remained unchecked until they were annihilated by the Mongols.

the Prophet and first wife of 'Ali. In 969, al-Mu'izz, the fourth Fatimid caliph, conquered Egypt and made Cairo his capital. The power of the Fatimids spread to Syria and Palestine, and for a century, was the most formidable in North Africa. After the death of the Caliph al-Mustansir in 1094, Fatimid power declined rapidly.

The theosophical system of Ismail'ism was organized and codified in Iraq and Persia in the eleventh century. It is based on an allegorical interpretation of the Qur'an and reflects the influence of Neo-Platonic ideas, as seen in the theory of expression. Between the tenth and eleventh centuries, two movements deriving from Ismail'ism appeared: the Nizari Isma'ilis and Druze sect.

The tradition of the Nizari imams extended to Persia, where Shah Fath granted them the title of Aga Khan (Master Prince) in 1834. Political intrigue forced the first Aga Khan into exile in India (1842) where he died forty years later. Today, Nizari Isma'ilis still exist in India, Syria, Iran, and Europe.

Shi'ism is not very

different from Sunni Islam in regards to worship and rituals. Besides the traditional feast days of Islam, the Shi'i commemorate the martyrdom at Karbala of the Imam Husayn and the descendants of the Prophet. This ceremony, celebrated during the first ten days of Muharram, the first month of the Islamic calendar, is a solemn festival of mourning and lamentation centered on the *ta'-ziyah*, passion plays depicting the tragic battle of Karbala. The birth of Husayn and that of his mother, Fatimah, are also celebrated.

In the ninth century, another Shi'i group, the Zaydiyya, named for Zayd ibn 'Ali, a descendent of 'Ali, helped shaped the doctrines of several small states, including Yemen and the states on the banks of the Caspian Sea. This group professes beliefs that are close to Sunnism but distinguishes itself by placing major importance on the principal of the imamate and Mu'tazilite theology. Present throughout Yemen and the Far East, today this branch counts more than six million followers.

Shi'i woman in prayer in front of the Mausoleum in Karbala. It is Shi'i custom to pray and ask for grace and pardon in the mausoleums where the imams are entombed.

The Shaykh school. In the eighteenth century the Shaykh school was formed. It is a synthesis of the Shi'i philosophy and the beliefs of certain Sufi brotherhoods. In 1844, Sayyid 'Ali Muhammad, born in 1821, a disciple of this school, pronounced

himself Bab (gateway to the Imam), and the mirror of the universal intelligence. Conflict between his two brothers divided the movement after his death. One of them, under the name of Baha'ollah, became the founder of Baha'ism, which professes

ideals of pacifism and universalism. Today, numerous followers of this movement live in the United States and several countries of Europe.

Master and disciple. Persian miniature (1560). Reza Abbasy Museum, Teheran. In Sufism, the master guides the disciple on the spiritual path.

Representing the esoteric tendencies in Islam, Sufism aspires to a personal, unmediated relationship, between man and God. The Sufis seek to withdraw from the formal and rigid practices of worship linked to the *shari'ah*. Their movement is characterized by dedication to the goal of purification of the soul and the knowledge of God. Sufis do not believe that submission to religious principles is the only way to attain this. Instead, they advocate an inner comprehension of the Islamic revelation in order to achieve the ideal of

tawhid (oneness with God). Full access to the mysteries of *tawhid* and deep knowledge of its meaning are activities reserved for the Sufi, who seeks to see God in His entirety.

The Sufi's ideal puts him in conflict with the *fuqaha* (scholars of the Islamic law), that is to say, there can be a divergence between respect for the *shari'ah* and the search for the *haqiqa* (truth).

Sufism aspires to a unique and absolute goal: total union with God. It pays little attention to the material and dogmatic preoccupations of Islamic doctrine, which promise rewards to the faithful as well as happiness in the hereafter. Freeing himself from worldly concerns, the Sufi considers his words and actions to be directly inspired by God, at a certain level of ecstasy, he becomes that which he has been searching for.

The *murid* (disciple) must be initiated by the *murshid* (master), who transmits to him the *baraka* (the divine power or blessing). Sufis teach that *baraka* has been passed

down from the Prophet through the *silsila* (the chain of authority). There are several schools of initiation, several *tariqah*, (paths) corresponding to particular *silsilas*. The great masters are the only receptacles of the authority needed to guarantee the authenticity of the chain. Sufism dates to the time of the Prophet, but the elaboration and formulation of the Sufi ideal, by the intermediation of inspired individuals, developed in secret, with small, exclusive meetings of disciples.

In the eighth century, before Sufi doctrine of Sufism had been fully articulated, Sufi practice consisted of reading aloud from the Qur'an during private meetings. It was not until later that Sufis began to practice *dhikr* (the repetitive chanting of one of the names of God, sometimes to music).

The teaching of Sufism took root in Baghdad during the middle of the ninth century. This became the center from which it spread. Abu-l-Qasim ibn Muhammad (d. 910), one

Hal, (the state of ecstasy). The longed-for union with the Divine, even if only temporary, cannot be expressed by words and is inaccessible to the ordinary man. The mystical state, ecstasy or *hal*, leads to an "immersion in the divine light."

The tariqah. By following the *tariqah* (the mystical path of Sufism), man endeavors to liberate himself from the illusions of multiplicity and lies in order to attain oneness, which is, for him, the sole hope of meriting salvation. The goal of Sufi

asceticism is the incarnation of *al-Insan al-Kamil* (the perfect man). God is One, and to become One, man must open himself to the universal.

of the representatives of the Baghdad school, is known for having articulated one of the most coherent doctrines of Sufism. His system of Islamic theosophy, aided by his profound and original intelligence, was never to be equaled. Foreign elements within the movement, essentially of a Christian or Persian nature, so profoundly modified Islamic conceptions, that some Sufis were rebuked for exceeding the strict regulations of the *shari'ah*.

Husayn ibn Mansur al-Hallaj (857–922), a Sufi of Persian origin was an important figure in early Sufism. Later, Sufism was continued in Persia by Shaykh Abu Sa'id Abi' l-Khair (967–1049), who laid the foundations of the symbolic interpretation of Sufi poetry. He was one of the first to establish a simple rule for his community.

Jalal al-Din Rumi (1207–1273), originally from present-day Afghanistan, created a large and diverse collection of poems in Persian. He was famous for his *masnavi*

(couplets), and, as the founder of the Mevlevi Sufi order, played a key role in the spread of Sufism to the Turkish-speaking world. Sufism's diverse currents of thought opened the door to individual initiative, giving birth to many different orders. Unfortunately, some of these became corrupt and lost sight of Sufism's ideal.

Evidence of the existence of organized Sufi orders can be found, starting in the twelfth and thirteenth centuries. The spiritual genealogy underpinning a Sufi *shaykh's* authority was called the *silsila*, probably borrowed from *isnad* (transmitter), one of the methods instituted to authenticate the validity of the *hadith*. In this way, the Sufi al-Khuldi (d. 959) traced the authenticity of his doctrine back to the early Sufi ascetic, Hasan al-Basri, and from Hasan to the Prophet himself, by the mediation of the Companion 'Anas ibn Malik. The Naqshbandi order traces its descent from the first caliph, Abu Bakr, and the Suhrawardi order from 'Umar, the second.

The *shaykh* is the leader of a Sufi brotherhood, and most of the order's spiritual activities occur in the *zawiyah*, his place of residence and teaching.

Sufism was an important vehicle for Islamic expansion and domination in northwest and sub-Saharan Africa. In the eleventh century, the Almoravid dynasty led a *jihad* aimed at the revitalization of orthodox Islam in these regions. In the twelfth century, the Almohad dynasty was influential in Spain in Morocco. Their leader, the Mahdi Ibn Turmart,

Sufi dance at Matmata, Tunisia. The Sufis aspire to a total union with God, through a sort of religious ecstasy, rather than the rewards of Paradise that are promised to those who respect Qur'anic laws.

Al-Hasan al-Basri.

An important early Sufi writer and teacher, Hasan al-Basri was born in 642 at Medina and died in 728 in Bassora. He based his teachings on the famous saying, "Behave yourself in this world as if it never existed, and with the other world as if you never have to leave it. O man, sell your present life for your future life and you will earn both, you will not lose either one or the other." Because of his fervent teaching, he is considered to be one of the founders of Sufism.

Rabia al-Adawiya

The origin of the doctrine of pure love, or love which is freely given, being the only love worthy of God, is attributed to the illustrious poetess Rabia al-Adawiya (721–801), who wrote during the first period of Islamic mysticism.

Page from The Conference of the Birds, *a work in verse of a spiritual nature by Farid al-Din 'Attar. Persian, 15th–16th centuries. Biblioteca Palatina, Parma.*

Below: *Wise-man in meditation. Moghul school (17th century). British Museum, London.*

imposed the *ach'arite*, orthodoxy of Sufi inspiration.

Abu Madyan, a Sufi saint born in Seville, is credited with the creation of the center of Sufi influence in North Africa in the twelfth century. His student was the great pantheistic theosophist Muhammad Muhyi-a-Din Akbar ibn Arabi (1165–1240) of Murcia, Spain. Abu al-Hasan ash-Shadhili (1196–1258), a disciple of Abu Madyan, was the founder of the Shadhili order. One of his disciples, Ibn Ata Allah of Alexandria (d. 1309) left a collection of maxims, *al-Hakim*, which is the fundamental text of the order.

The Naqshbandi order, founded in the fourteenth century in Bukhara by Muhammad Baha'a-Din Naqshband (1317–1389), is one of the largest Sufi brotherhoods. Its influence extends today throughout Central Asia, Turkey, the Muslim Orient, and Europe. An orthodox order, it attracted a cultured elite by its austerity. It forbids dancing, music, and all uncontrolled forms of *dhikr*.

The Sufis quickly succeeded in reformulating the traditional meaning of *khawf*, (fear), and of *radja*, (hope), by giving them a new esoteric dimension. For the Sufis, they become the two principles that permit access to the true knowledge of God: the annihilation of *fana* (finiteness, that is, self annihilation) and *baqa* (survival in God), the most advanced state of Sufi practice.

Devoted to ascetic practices and the purification of the soul, Sufism is exclusively oriented toward the goal of walking in God's path. Spiritual progress, called *mudjahada*, is attained by passing through higher and higher stages called *maqamat*. The heart of the Sufi vision is *al-hubb al-ilahi* (the love for the Divine), on which rests the theory of knowledge and existence.

The Sufi believes that love is a resolution. As such, the love of God for His creatures is given out of His will to love and is the reason for the grace granted to men. The word "love" is frequently met with in the Qur'an. The Qur'an describes the downward movement of divine love towards God's servant as well as the love that ascends from the servant towards God, and the "exchange" between the two. "Say, 'If you love God then follow me that God may love you and forgive your faults...'" (Qur'an 3: 31).

The Egyptian Dou l-Noun al-Misri (796–856) added to this new conception of divine love the notion of *uns'* (shared intimacy). Intimacy with God comes from the desire to serve Him with a total selflessness, because of the joy that the Beloved gives to the heart of he who contemplates Him.

Sufis, over time, developed an increasingly esoteric language, the sense of which escapes non-initiates. The *shatahat*, (swoonings) were used against Sufis by their enemies, because they were seen to oppose the *shari'ah*. The *shatahat* are the visible expression of the two important elements of *fana'*: *zawal al-hidjab*,

The Qadiri order. Currently, one of the most important orders of Sufis is the Qadiri, named for the man who inspired it, 'Abd al-Qadir al-Jilani. He was born in 1078 in the region of Jilan in Persia, and died in Baghdad in 1166. Al-Jilani's teaching was an urgent call to exalt charity and duty toward one's neighbor above the consideration of temporal interests. Founded in Baghdad, this brotherhood spread into North Africa, sub-Saharan Africa, northern Turkey, and in the East as far as Indochina.

The Suhrawardi order. Developed around the doctrines of Shihab al-Din al-Suhrawardi (1145–1234), this order spread to Afghanistan and India. It was inspired in the nineteenth century by the theory of the illumination of the order of Sanusiyya.

(unveiling) and *ghalabat al-shuhud* (the priority of contemplation).

The Sufi is opposed to anything that mediates between the seeker and God, because each mediation is a reminder that union has not yet been achieved. The first of the mediations that he must overcome is the *shari'ah*. This is only possible if the Tradition is interpreted differently, in a way which could be called "interior", by calling it the *haqiqa*, (truth). In the same way, Islamic liturgy interpreted in a symbolic sense takes on a new esoteric dimension. This way of thinking, already noticeable with the first Sufis, like Rabia ben Ismael al-Adiwiya, Marud al-Kharkhi (d. 815), and others, ignited condemnation and severe reprisals from traditionalists.

In Sufism, the act of worship is dissociated from all thoughts of reward. Its only goal is knowledge of the Beloved. The Sufi neither fears Hell nor longs for Paradise. To reach the second stage of *fana'*, the contemplation of the Divine, or *al-shuhud*, the

servant of God must free himself from all attachment to his individual being in order to achieve an annihilation of self. This mystical ideal contributed to Sufism's conspicuousness, compared to the traditional practices of Islam. Even though Sufis place great emphasis on discretion, ecstasy is a state that is hard to disguise. Their passionate attachment to ecstasy and to *shatahat* has always been a reason for the hostility toward and rejection of Sufism by traditionalists.

The goal of the mystical technique of the Sufi is the *ma'rifah* (knowledge). When the Sufi attains it, he sees nothing other than God and is entirely subsumed in Him. This inner knowledge fills his heart. It is a state of "meditation, of inner observation", and at its culmination, the self is obliterated, withdrawn outside of the world and body.

In the Sufi doctrine, the renunciation of the world and the practice of devotion are considered as the first steps towards *tasawwuf* (asceticism).

Detachment from the material world comes from agreement without reserve to the will of God, and from satisfying oneself with his favors.

Whirling dervishes. For this Sufi order (Mevlevi), the dance serves to reach a state of ecstasy.

The Rifa'iya order.
Ahmad al-Rifa'i (d. 1182), founded the Rifa'iya at Bassora in Iraq. This brotherhood exists in Egypt, Turkey, and Asia.

The Badawi order.
Venerated as one of the greatest saints, Ahmad al-Badawi (d. 1276) was the founder of the Badawi order, which introduced certain elements from pre-Islamic Egypt in its practices.

The Mevlevi
The largest and most refined of the popular Turkish orders, it was founded by the poet Jalal-al Din Rumi (1207–1273). Its followers, the "whirling dervishes", and the Rumi's poetry have become famous in the West.

Room of a caldarium in the palace of Comares. Alhambra, Granada, Spain.

Below: *Ceramic tile (end of 13th century). Museum of Oriental Art, Rome.*

The confrontation and cultural exchange between Islam and Europe took place in the Mediterranean basin. The Arab conquest of Spain may have shocked the Christian world, but for Muslims it was part of the continuity of the Islamic migration that began during the life of the Prophet. For the nomadic Arabs, the habits of migration and raiding established traditions that necessarily included violence. With the advent of Islam, these customs survived by being channeled into the *jihad* for the path of God.

The energy that the tribes expended in internecine battles was then focused outwards to the benefit of *dar al-Islam*, (the lands of Islam). The attacks were first directed against Iraq and Syria, then against Iran and Egypt. The Muslims' growing excitement paralleled their many victories and their accumulation of booty.

In the beginning, the *jihad* was directed against polytheists and Jewish tribes who had broken their pact with the Prophet. During the period of Islamic expansion, the *jihad* was not focused on forcing the conquered peoples to yield to Islam. Special treatment was always reserved for *ahl al-kitab* (people of the Book). Since the beginning, Islam had granted them the status of *dhimmis* (protected), the name given to the *muhahiddun* (monotheists). The *muhahiddun* were granted a degree of independence and freedom of worship, within the Islamic state, on the condition that they pay a tax, the *jizya*, in return for the state's protection.

In the Iberian peninsula, power was vested in the hands of governors appointed by the Caliph of Damascus, until the bloody fall of the Umayyad dynasty. With the advent of the Abbasid dynasty (750–1258), the political situation in Andalusia changed radically.

'Abd al-Rahman ibn Mu'awiya and one of his brothers were the only members of the Umayyad dynasty to escape the massacre perpetrated by the Abbassids. At first, they took refuge in North Africa. 'Abd al-Rahman was able to profit from the conflict between the Kalb faction against the Qays faction, that ruled Andalusia. Finally, in 756, al-Rahman's struggle

The Arabs and southern Italy.
During the long period of the Arab presence, Sicily experienced economic and social development, profited from agricultural techniques perfected in the Arab world, and developed a refined culture and art, of which magnificent examples remain. In the period of decline that followed, the Arab presence was reduced to a band of rebels that were finally deported to Lucera, in Apulia by Frederick II. During the height of their influence, in the ninth and tenth centuries, the Arabs crossed into the south of Italy (Calabria, Apulia, Campania and Basilicata). Their incursions led in two cases, at Bari and at Taranto, to the creation short-lived emirates.

against the Andalusian governor brought him to the gates of Córdoba, where he emerged victorious. At twenty-six years old, al-Rahman made his triumphant entry into the town that was to become the capital of his emirate.

After having brought peace to the land, 'al-Rahman, called *al-Dhakhil* (the immigrant), laid the foundations of a completely independent emirate.

The strength of the emirate was considerably reinforced under Hisham, son and successor of 'Abd al-Rahman. In Andalusia, as in the rest of the Islamic west, the Sunni *Maliki* school of law was imposed. It contributed greatly to Islam by producing a series of excellent scholars and jurists, that constituted one of the most solid pillars of the Umayyad regime.

Under 'Abd al-Rahman II (792–852), the organization of the state was inspired by the Abbasid model, which was itself based on the Byzantine court. In fact, political exchanges between Córdoba and Constant-inople were frequent.

Andalusia's growing cosmpolitanism was, in large measure, due to the curiosity and diversity of personal interests of 'Abd al-Rahman II. An enthusiastic student of religion, educated in the jurisprudence of the *Maliki* school, he surrounded himself with musicians, poets, philosophers, and astrologers. Among the most famous were Abbas ibn Ifirnas (d. 888), Yahia al-Ghazal (774–864) and Ziryab (d. 845). Abbas ibn Ifirnas, an experimental philosopher built himself a harness of feathers and silk. Wearing this contraption, he threw himself off a hill and actually accomplished a long, straight flight from which he emerged unharmed. Yahia was given the name *al-Ghazal* (the gazelle) because of his physical grace. He was a poet and author of stinging satires that did not spare the emir himself. The Iraqi Ziryab was a celebrated and very original personality. He became the arbiter of taste for the Spanish Muslim society. He introduced the fashion of wearing white during the summer and pastels in the spring and was the creator of the ceremonial rules for banquets. He was also a skilled musician and a renowned gourmet.

The Caliph 'Abd al-Rahman III (890–961), called *al-Nazir* (the victorious), played an important role in the transmission of classical learning. Around 948, envoys of Constantinople brought Greek copies of Dioscorides' book on medicine, and works by the Latin historian, Paulus Orosius, to Andalusia. Al-Nazir oversaw their translation into Arabic, entrusting them to the

Andalusia.

At the apogee of Andalusian culture, under the caliphate of Córdoba, Muslim civilization experienced its most important intellectual and artistic achievements. The prestige of the Córdoban state was widespread. The money of the emirate was minted in the Dar as-sikka, the interior of the Alcazar palace. Precious fabrics bearing the name of the emir were woven in the *tiraz* (creative workshops). State monopolies were founded, and commercial relations with the East, neighboring North Africa, and the European world in general multiplied.

Wood ceiling of the Palatine chapel of Palermo (c. 1143). Work of the Fatimid school, example of Islamic art in Sicily.

Below: *Miniature by al-Wasity representing the interior of a library (1237). Bibliothèque nationale, Paris.*

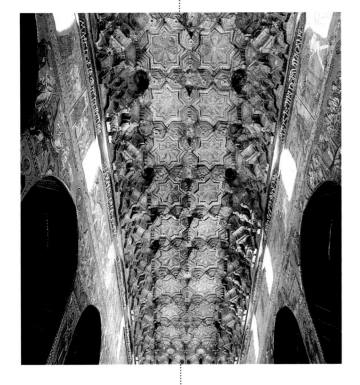

Christian monk Nicolas and to the Jewish scholar Hasdai ibn Shaqrit.

The predilection of Caliph al-Hakim II, son of 'Abd al-Rahman III, for the arts and sciences contributed to their unprecedented flowering in Andalusia. This period also witnessed a population explosion that suggests it was one of economic well-being. Córdoba at this time counted a half-million inhabitants.

The Umayyad caliphate officially ended on November 30, 1031. Exhausted by the country's intolerable governor and by the ambitions of greedy and incapable politicians, the bourgeoisie citizens pronounced themselves in favor of the installation of a republic, ruled by a council of leading townspeople. In fact, the demise of the regime had been assured three weeks earlier by the sack of Córdoba by the Berbers. This event resulted in the murder of Caliph Hisham III (1029–1031) and the dispersion of the country's irreplaceable literary heritage.

Because there was no leader capable of unifying the region, Andalusia was divided into numerous republics, principalities, and kingdoms, controlled by aristocrats, men of law, or even soldiers, whose unrestrained ambitions were greater than their aptitude to govern. Heads of regional kingdoms, called *tawa'if,* began to emerge. These were usually Arabs, Berbers or the slaves who had won their independence at the end of the Amirid dictatorship.

Andalusia had become a mosaic of petty principalities.

In 1236, Ferdinand III of Castille conquered Córdoba. On January 6, 1492, with the triumphal entry of the "very Catholic" kings, the *reconquista* was achieved. The same year, the immense Jewish colonywas expelled from the kingdom. In 1609, Philip III signed a decree banishing all Muslim subjects from the land.

Arab poetry and Western poetry.

The term *muwashshah* literally means "a pearl necklace of two strands of different colors." The term describes a poetic genre composed of five to seven stanzas or more, with clever combinations of rhymes.

The inventor of this poetic form was Muqaddam al-Qabra (840–912), a blind Andalusian artist. At the beginning, the *muwashshah* were written in classical Arabic by poets such as, Ahmad ibn 'Abd Rabbihi (860–940), the principal Andalusian poet, Ibn Abbadah al-Qazzaz (d.

The library of al-Hakim. In a country renowned for its high level of education and its love of books, the personal library of al-Hakim III was the ultimate symbol of the golden age of the Córdoban caliphate. The impressive quantity of manuscripts,

more than four hundred thousand volumes in several languages, was only later equaled by the magnitude of the library of Ibn Abbas, the rich wazir of the prince of Almeria.

1095), Lisan ad-din ibn al-Khatib (1313–1374). Later, the long poems ended with a short repetition of verse or couplet in the vernacular, called a *kharja*. This form of strophic poetry can be considered as the most characteristic and authentic expression of Andalusian Arabic art.

Its reputation as noble literature was confirmed by its greatest and most famous representative, Ibn Qazam (1108–1160). Traveling from town to town, he passed his life singing the praises of different governors of the states unified under the domination of the Morabitoun. The recurring themes of his poems are ..., love, and the ...uality so characteristic ...is temperament.

The *muwashshah* is ...ated to another type of ...rnacular composition, ...lled *zajal*. Among the precursors of this style are Abu Yusuf ar-Ramadi (926–1013), Said ibn 'Abd Rabbihi (d. 954) and Ibn Ma'as-Sama, who died in Malaga in 1031. According to Julian Ribera, a specialist in the Romance vernacular literature, we owe the birth

of European poetry, starting with the *dolce stil nuovo*, to the diffusion of this type of Arab poetry through Europe, particularly in Spain and Sicily. The use of this poetic style in the poems of the first troubadours can be found in popular Sicilian, Italian and European poetry, in the religious poetry of the Franciscans of the thirteenth and fourteenth centuries, and in the songs and the carnival chants of Florence of the fifteenth century.

In Spain, the art of the *zajal* is found in the works of the poets Alphonse X in the thirteenth century, and Villa Sandino, and Juan del Encina in fifteenth and sixteenth centuries. This genre of poetry had interesting formal properties, and its subjects and themes were to have a profound influence on European poetry. It gave rise to the conventions of courtly love that were to revolutionize medieval European literature.

Courtly love is the principal subject of the book *al-Zahrah*, The Rose, by Abu Bakr az-Zahairi, who died in Baghdad in

910. Later, the Andalusian writer and philosopher Abu Muhammad 'Ali ibn Hazm (994–1064) proposed a theoretical treatise on love in his *Tawq al-hamama*, The Necklace of the Dove. His influence is noticeable in the poetry of Dante and Petrarch. The construction of the sonnet is very close to the *muwashshah* genre.

Fragment of a poem by Ibn Zamrack in the room of Dos Hermanas, Alhambra, Granada, Spain. Andalusian Arabic poetry is the source for several Western poetic genres.

Below: *The lovers. Detail of a Persian painting of the 15th century. Florence, private collection.*

Common elements. The connection between Romantic poetry, the *muwashshah* and the *zajal*, rests upon similarities like the presence in the two genres of the figures of "voyeur", "gossip", "jealous one" and "fellow." The reader is cast in the role of

the lovers' confidant. The lover's name was never mentioned; he was only depicted as "my lord" or "one's fellow." Motifs common in European literature such as love at first sight, the frightening away of the loved woman, the anguish of true love

which culminates in depression, insomnia and sometimes even death, and the mourning for the beloved who leaves for war, were already present in Arab poetry before they arrived in Europe.

Glossary

Adhan: Muslim call to prayer.

Ahl al-kitab: "People of the Book", the followers of the religions of the written Revelation: Jews, Christians, Zoroastrians.

Arkan: Pillars of Islam. These are Islam's five fundamental precepts: the profession of faith, prayer, charity, fasting, and pilgrimage.

'Achura: The tenth day of the month of Muharram, on which fasting is recommended. It coincides with the commemoration of the assassination of Husayn, son of 'Ali.

Bismillah ar-Rahman ar-Raheem: "In the name of Allah, most benevolent, ever-merciful"; this is the formula which opens all of the *surah* of the Qur'an. It is said before the reading of documents, speeches and the performance of all religious acts by the believer.

Fatihah: "The Prologue", "the Opening"; name of the first *surah* of the Qur'an. This is the most commonly used text of the Holy Book.

Fiqh: The science of Islamic jurisprudence, to which the Muslim is subject. It legally classifies all actions according to values that range from required to forbidden.

Ghusl: Total ablution of the body, necessary to re-establish the state of purity that is required to carry out ritual acts, used in cases where the believer is in a state of great impurity.

Hadith: "Narrative", "story", or "anecdote". The *hadiths* contain the words, works, and behaviors of the Prophet. They were passed on orally.

Hajj: The great pilgrimage to Mecca, which every Muslim must carry out at least once during his or her life, during a specific period of the year.

Hanif: Those who, during the pre-Islamic period, did not accept polytheism, nor subscribe to Christianity or Judaism. Later, this term was used to describe anyone who believed in one sole God.

Haram: The term signifies "holy" and "forbidden"; it was originally used to define the sacred quality of the land surrounding Mecca.

'Ibadat: In the *shari'ah*, the group of physical acts of worship by which man enters into a relationship with God.

Ijma': "Consensus", in Islamic law, the unanimous agreement of scholars, in conformity to the *shari'ah*, on important subjects. The third source of Islamic law.

Ijtihad: "Creative thought of the individual", the use of reason in the study of the Qur'an and the *sunnah*.

Imam: "Appointed", "head", "guide." Among the different meanings, the most common is he who leads congregational prayer in the mosque.

Isma'iliyyah: A branch of Shi'a. Its name derives from Isma'il, recognized by the Shi'i as the last legitimate imam.

Imamiyyah: A Shi'i Muslim community that awaits the return of the twelfth Imam, Muhammad al-Mahdi, who disappeared in 874.

Jihad: "Struggle", the duty of Muslims to take up arms "on the path of God." It is considered an obligation by the community, but is not one of the five Pillars. *Jihad* also has a figurative meaning: the inner struggle to fight against temptation and submit to the Will of God.

Jizya: The tax required of non-Muslim residents of the Islamic state.

Ka'bah: The cube-shaped, holy edifice situated at the center of Mecca. Islamic tradition attributes its construction to Abraham.

Khulafa' ar-Raschidun: The "Rightly-Guided Caliphs". The first four orthodox caliphs, successors of the Prophet.

Khutba: The religious sermon preached by the imam who leads the Friday congregational prayer in the mosque.

Madhhab: "Method" or "rite"; designates the four schools of Sunni Muslim law: *Hanafi*, *Maliki*, *Shafi'I*, and *Hanbali*.

Madrassah: Qur'anic school. Generally held in or beside a mosque, it teaches the *fiqh* and the Qur'an.

Mihrab: Arched, concave niche in a wall of a mosque, indicating the direction of Mecca.

Mu'amalat: In the *shari'ah*, this refers to the sphere of relations between individuals (as opposed to the relationship between an individual and God).

Mufti: Supreme judicial figure, who has the authority to make a legal opinion (*fatwa*) regarding a point of Islamic law.

Qiblah: The direction of Mecca toward which the faithful turn during prayer.

Qiyas: "Analogical deduction"; the fourth source of Islamic law.

Qur'an: For Muslims, it is the largest of miracles, inimitable, the eternal word of Allah, co-eternal with God and uncreated. It was revealed to Muhammad, who was the physical intermediary of the divine Revelation.

Ramadan: Ninth month of the Muslim lunar calendar, during which the Qur'an was revealed to the Prophet, and the month of the annual fast.

Sadaqa: Voluntary charity, not regulated by precise rules like the *zakat*.

Salafiyya: Reformist Islamic movement starting in Egypt between the eighteenth and nineteenth centuries. Its goal was to purge all foreign elements from Islamic tradition.

Salat: The second Pillar of Islam, the canonical prayer, made five times daily at prescribed times.

Sawm: The fourth Pillar of Islam; the fast during the month of Ramadan. The *sawm* is required of all Muslim adults in good health.

Sa'yi: The procession that the pilgrims make seven times between the hills of Safa and Marwa during the great pilgrimage.

Shari'ah: Part of the Islamic doctrine that Muslims consider as fundamental to the faith; the law which regulates all actions, private or public.

Shahadah: The profession of faith, first Pillar of Islam.

Shi'a: The party of 'Ali, cousin and son-in-law of the Prophet; the Muslims who follow the Shi'a are called "Shi'i".

Shura: Council established by the Caliph 'Umar, composed of the Companions of the Prophet.

Sufism: The mystical branch of Islam.

Sunnah: "Behavior"; one of the four sources of Islamic theology and law, along with the Qur'an, the *ijma'* and the *qiyas*. The sources of the *sunnah* are the *hadiths*.

Surah: Each of the 114 chapters which composes the Qur'an.

Takbir: The *Allahu Akbar* formula, "God is Great", said by the faithful carrying out certain ritual acts.

Tariqah: "The mystical path", designating the mystical Muslim brotherhoods.

Tawaf: Circumambulation carried out by the faithful during pilgrimage composed of seven consecutive cycles, in counter-clockwise direction, around the Ka'bah.

'Ulama': Plural of *'alim*, a term which designates the scholars who are versed in the knowledge of the Qur'an.

Umma: "Community" or "nation", designating a group of Muslims, without any ethnic or cultural distinctions.

'Umrah: A minor pilgrimage to Mecca, which can be made at any time of the year.

Wahhabiyyah: Rigid Sunni movement founded by Muhammad ibn 'Abd al-Wahhab in central Arabia in the middle of the eighteenth century.

Wudu': Minor ablution bringing a state of purity necessary to carry out acts of worship.

Zakat: "Almsgiving tithe", the third Pillar of Islam.

Zaydiyya: Muslim Shi'i sect of moderate leanings, founded by Zayd ibn 'Ali, who died in 740.

Islam in the world

Currently, the spread of Islam is not limited to countries of the Islamic world. Many Muslims live in Europe and on the American continent. All-embracing, Islam is the largest religion after Christianity. There are around 840,000,000 Muslims, 17% of the world's population.

Middle and Far East: 550,000,000; Africa: 230,000,000; Asian republics and ex-Soviet Union: 45,000,000; Europe: 9,000,000; American continent: 2,000,000.

The most populous Islamic country is Indonesia. Its 147,000,000 Muslims represent 82% of the population; following are Pakistan (80,000,000, 97%), India (80,000,000, 12%), Bangladesh (75,000,000, 80%), Turkey (99%) and Egypt (85%). There are 55,000,000 Muslims in China. In the Middle-East and North Africa, Muslims represent around 90% of the population.

There are around 700,000,000 Sunni and 90,000,000 Shi'i in the world. The Shi'i are the majority in Iran (90%), Iraq (more than 55%), Lebanon, Azerbaijan, Oman and Yemen (50% are Zaydi Shi'i). All of the other Islamic countries have a Sunni majority.

In the Balkan Peninsula there is a large Muslim presence in Bosnia-Herzegovina (around 44% of the population) as in Albania (70%). Other countries of Europe that are home to a Muslim community include France (5% of the population) and Germany (3%).

The Islamic calendar

The Muslim calendar is calculated on the lunar year, composed of an average of 354 days, divided into twelve months: Muharram, Safar, Rabi' al-Awal, Rabi' at-Thani, Jamad al-Awal, Jamad at-Thani, Rajab, Sha'ban, Ramadan, Shawal, Dou al-Qidah, Dhu al-Hijjah.

The beginning of each month is determined by the phase of the new moon, each month having a variable length. On the twenty-ninth day of each month, the Muslims await the rising of the new moon. If it is visible, the next month starts the following day. If it is not, the following day becomes the thirtieth day of the current month.

The calculation of years begins at the conventional date of the *Hijrah*, the 16th of July, 622.